PRAYERS
FOR
PEACE
OF MIND

Other Works by Holley Gerth

PRAYERS FOR PEACE OF MIND

Scripture and Encouragement
for Days of Anxiety, Worry, and Stress

HOLLEY GERTH

Revell

a division of Baker Publishing Group
Grand Rapids, Michigan

Published by Revell
a division of Baker Publishing Group
Grand Rapids, Michigan
RevellBooks.com

Printed in China

Library of Congress Cataloging-in-Publication Control Number: 2025002571
ISBN 9780800747312 (cloth)
ISBN 9781493451036 (ebook)

Unless otherwise indicated, Scripture quotations are from the *Holy Bible*, New Living Translation. Copyright © 1996, 2004, 2015 by Tyndale House Foundation. Used by permission of Tyndale House Publishers, Carol Stream, Illinois 60188. All rights reserved.

Scripture quotations labeled AMP are from the Amplified Bible. Copyright © 2015 by The Lockman Foundation. Used by permission. www.lockman.org

Scripture quotations labeled CSB are from the Christian Standard Bible®. Copyright © 2017 by Holman Bible Publishers. Used by permission. Christian Standard Bible® and CSB® are federally registered trademarks of Holman Bible Publishers.

Scripture quotations labeled ESV are from The Holy Bible, English Standard Version® (ESV®). Copyright © 2001 by Crossway, a publishing ministry of Good News Publishers. Used by permission. All rights reserved. ESV Text Edition: 2016

Scripture quotations labeled NIV are from the Holy Bible, New International Version®, NIV®. Copyright © 1973, 1978, 1984, 2011 by Biblica, Inc.® Used by permission of Zondervan. All rights reserved worldwide. www.zondervan.com. The "NIV" and "New International Version" are trademarks registered in the United States Patent and Trademark Office by Biblica, Inc.®

Scripture quotations labeled NKJV are from the New King James Version®. Copyright © 1982 by Thomas Nelson. Used by permission. All rights reserved.

This book contains material adapted from *What Your Soul Needs for Stressful Times* (Revell, 2021) and *What Your Mind Needs for Anxious Moments* (Revell, 2022).

Cover design by Mumtaz Mustafa

Interior design by William Overbeeke

Baker Publishing Group publications use paper produced from sustainable forestry practices and postconsumer waste whenever possible.

25 26 27 28 29 30 31   7 6 5 4 3 2 1

CONTENTS

INTRODUCTION

We all have anxious moments and stressful thoughts. Maybe yours happen when you watch the news, worry about a loved one, get ready for a big meeting, or stare at the ceiling in the night thinking about the future. Your heart might pound, your mind may race, or your sleep could get interrupted.

Your anxiety and stress might even make you wonder if your faith is weak or something is wrong with you. But neither is true. Anxiety and stress are an inevitable part of being human, but they don't have to control your mind. You really can live with more contentment and less worry, more inner peace and less fear, more joy and less stress.

God alone is big enough to carry your burdens, work out all your worries, and transform your anxious moments into soul-deep peace. His love for you is endless, his grace complete, and his plan for your life full of hope. He can set you free from anxiety one moment, one thought, one step at a time—starting right now.

God Meets You Where You Are Today

> Then the LORD God called to the man,
> "Where are you?"
>   He replied, "I heard you walking in
> the garden, so I hid."
>
> Genesis 3:9–10

God is asking you today, "Where are you?"
No matter the answer, he already knows.
What he's really asking is, "Are you ready to let
me meet you where you are today?"

God wants to free you from stress or anxiety,
deliver you from fear, and bring you to a new
place of knowing in an even deeper way how
much you're loved.

You never have to hide your emotions or what
you're experiencing from him. You don't have to
say "I'm fine" one more time. You are not alone

in anything you go through in this life. Even now, God is calling to your heart. He welcomes you even in your most anxious moments.

I created each of the pages in this book to be a sacred place where you and God can meet. He is inviting you to show up as you are and receive whatever you need right now.

God, thank you for your great tenderness toward me. I'm so grateful you want to meet me where I am today. I need your help with my anxiety. Amen.

God Sees Everything in Your Life

> But God heard the boy crying, and the angel of God called to Hagar from heaven, "Hagar, what's wrong? Do not be afraid!"
>
> Genesis 21:17

When we're anxious about those we love, it feels as if their well-being depends on us. We have to keep them safe. We have to ensure they make the right choices. We need to control what happens. But the story of Hagar and Ishmael in Genesis reminds us that God is ultimately in charge of those we love. He is their Protector. He is their Provider. He is the one who will meet them in the dry, desert places where there seems to be no hope.

Instead of being anxious, we can take our concerns to God. Then we can comfort, encourage, and be there for that person. We can't control the results of the situation, but we can choose how we will be present in the relationship. Worrying can't change what will happen, but prayerfully walking with someone through whatever comes their way can make all the difference.

God, thank you for loving the people in my life even more than I do. I'm especially concerned about _____. Please take care of this person today in ways only you can. Amen.

God's Love and Promises Are Real

Lead me by your truth and teach me,
for you are the God who saves me.
All day long I put my hope in you.

Psalm 25:5

Anxiety often tells us, "If people really knew who *you* are . . ."

You wouldn't be loved.

You'd never be accepted.

You'd be alone and rejected.

So we act like everything is fine, overachieve to prove our worth, overspend to keep up with our neighbors, or simply never dare to let ourselves be deeply known.

How do we stop repeating these patterns? *We return to the truth.* We can choose to do so as an act of faith. We remember we don't have to cultivate an image to impress people, because we were created in the image of God.

You are already loved.

You are already accepted.

God will never leave or forsake you.

We don't have to pretend. God invites us to entrust our real, imperfect, in-progress selves to him.

God, remind me that I'm loved, I'm accepted, and you are with me always. You get the final word in my life, and what you speak is always true. Amen.

God Works
on Your Behalf

You intended to harm me, but God intended it all for good.

Genesis 50:20

Jesus tells us, "Here on earth you will have many trials and sorrows. But take heart, because I have overcome the world" (John 16:33). Although Joseph lived many centuries before Jesus, we still see this truth in his life. Joseph took heart by continuing to trust God was at work even when all the outward evidence seemed to indicate otherwise. He saw beyond what was possible from a human perspective and believed God would get him through whatever came.

Because Joseph persevered, God used him to save the lives of thousands of people, including his family. What seemed like pointless pain served a greater purpose. Whatever you're going through today, whatever anxiety is trying to say, God is still working in your life. Even when you can't yet see his hand, he's accomplishing his good plan to give you hope and a future.

God, thank you for working all things together for good in my life. When anxiety tries to lie to me, help me hold on to truth and remember how much you love me. Amen.

God Makes
a Way for You

Don't be afraid. Just stand still and
watch the LORD rescue you today. . . .
The LORD himself will fight for you. Just
stay calm.

Exodus 14:13–14

When anxiety tries to overcome us, it can
feel much like it did for the Israelites
as Pharaoh's army chased them after they
left Egypt. We look at overwhelming circumstances, and suddenly questions come to our
minds. "Why is this happening to me? What
have I gotten myself into? I should have seen
this coming!" In those moments, we can follow
Moses's example.

First, he acknowledges the fear the Israelites
are experiencing. Then Moses offers truth—
the Lord will rescue the people. Most of us

have heard the story of what happens next. God parts the waters of the Red Sea and the Israelites walk through it. The outcome in our lives might not be as dramatic, but the truth of this story is the same: God will make a way. He will lead us out of anxiety and into peace. He will guide us beyond fear and into courage. He will replace our questions with the certainty of his unfailing love.

God, nothing is too difficult for you. No circumstance is too challenging, no obstacle too big, no situation beyond your solutions. When anxiety leads me to question the future, help me trust that you are working in ways beyond what I can even imagine. Amen.

God Gives You a New Song

I will sing to the LORD,
　　for he has triumphed gloriously;
he has hurled both horse and rider
　　into the sea.
The LORD is my strength and my song;
　　he has given me victory.

Exodus 15:1–2

When I look at the discoveries made about the human brain and nervous system, I feel a sense of awe. Only God could create every part of us so perfectly, giving us everything we need to not just survive but thrive.

It turns out that when we sing, it stimulates and strengthens our vagus nerve. Counselors Yana Hoffman and Dr. Hank Davis explain, "The 'wandering' or vagus nerve is the longest cranial nerve in the body. It connects the brain and the gut, lungs, and heart. And it plays a critical role in helping us 'rest and digest.' Increasing the tone of the vagus nerve enables our body to relax faster after experiencing stress."[1]

Singing can not only help us recover from stress but also give us more courage and holy calm in anxiety-provoking situations.

All throughout Scripture, people sing—in times of difficulty, joy, sorrow, victory, fear, and everything in between.

God, you are the song of my heart, the focus of my worship, the one who causes words of praise to rise up within me. Give me a new song to sing, one of calm and courage. Amen.

God Can Handle Your Questions

The angel of the LORD appeared to him and said, "Mighty hero, the LORD is with you!"

"Sir," Gideon replied, "if the LORD is with us, why has all this happened to us? And where are all the miracles our ancestors told us about? Didn't they say, 'The LORD brought us up out of Egypt'?"

Judges 6:12–13

One of the biggest signs of anxiety is endless questioning. What if? How will this work out? Can I do this? We think our questions have to go away or be fully answered before God can use us. But the story of Gideon shows us God can handle our questions. What matters is that we take steps of obedience *even as we're still questioning.*

When we find ourselves in a place of fear like Gideon, we can bring God our concerns, hurts, and worries, and the ways we wish things were different. He's a safe place for all our emotions and uncertainty. Then he says to us, as he did to Gideon, "Go with the strength you have" (v. 14). Why? Because the strength we have is *his* strength. We may always question what's going on around us, but we can also always trust the One who lives within us.

God, there is so much I don't understand. When I want to hide and uncertainty surrounds me, give me the strength and courage to do what you are asking of me anyway. I choose to trust you. Amen.

God Still Has
a Plan for You

> May the LORD, the God of Israel, under whose wings you have come to take refuge, reward you fully for what you have done.

> Ruth 2:12

It appears Ruth came to the Jewish faith through Naomi's son, and she seems to have an inexplicable strength beneath her grief. She weeps as Naomi does but not without hope. She worries but also worships, has tough days and yet persists in putting one foot in front of the other. Naomi has become hard and bitter; Ruth inexplicably remains softhearted and open.

We all find ourselves acting like each of these women at one point or another. What matters is that we recognize when we're slipping into bitterness. In those moments, what we often need is a friend, family member, wise counselor, or other support person—a Ruth. God himself is always with us too, especially when we feel alone.

He is always working out an unseen plan, even when we don't understand. Anxiety tells us, "It's all over." But faith, and the Ruths in our lives, remind us, "God isn't finished with your story yet."

God, when it seems easier to choose bitter instead of better, give me the strength to keep trusting you have a plan beyond what I can understand. Give me the courage to reach out to a Ruth when I need to, and show me who needs me to be a Ruth to them as well. Amen.

God Defeats the Giants in Your Life

David replied to the Philistine, "You come to me with sword, spear, and javelin, but I come to you in the name of the LORD of Heaven's Armies."

1 Samuel 17:45

For the Israelites, everything changes when David shows up at the battlefield because David brings something with him that no one else has—a different perspective. Saul, the Israelites, and even Goliath see this as a human battle. But David views it as a spiritual one.

With only a sling and a small stone, David took down a giant. What seemed impossible from an earthly viewpoint became reality when approached with an eternal perspective. Anxiety can make us see only what's possible within our human limitations. But we, like David, can look beyond those limitations to what only God can do.

Anxiety says, "You can't."

Faith says, "God can."

Anxiety says, "You won't."

Faith says, "God will."

We are never in the battle alone—and that makes all the difference.

God, thank you that I never have to face anything without you. When anxiety tries to tell me the giant in my life is going to win, bring me back to the truth of who you are again. You will rescue me. You will conquer the giants in my life. This is your battle. Amen.

God Cares for You

But Elijah said to her, "Don't be afraid!
. . . For this is what the LORD, the God of
Israel, says: There will always be flour
and olive oil left in your containers until
the time when the LORD sends rain and
the crops grow again!"

1 Kings 17:13–14

In challenging times, anxiety tells us, "You have
to take care of yourself." It feels like it's all up to
us. It can seem as if we're down to our last bit of
courage, hope, and strength. In that moment
God may ask us to do something that makes
no sense at all. He might send someone into
our lives to serve. He may invite us to tell our
hard, brave story.

What will we choose? When we dare to trust,
we can discover our own version of the story in
1 Kings 17. Yours might sound like this: "There

was always enough courage and strength left in her heart, just as the Lord had promised."

We serve a God of abundance. With him, there is always more grace, more love, more of whatever we need in any moment.

God, thank you for being the source of what my heart needs today. When anxiety tries to tell me there's not enough, remind me you are a God of abundance. I'm not on my own, trying to take care of everything myself. You are with and for me always. Amen.

God Understands You're Human

Then the angel of the LORD came again and touched [Elijah] and said, "Get up and eat some more, or the journey ahead will be too much for you."

1 Kings 19:7

Haven't we all had moments of irrational anxiety and exhaustion, *even when we've just seen God work in our lives*? God's response to this situation is so reassuring. He didn't rebuke Elijah; instead, he sent an angel with snacks and water while Elijah took a nap. God didn't reason with Elijah when he was physically depleted. Instead, because he created our bodies, God knows sometimes what we need when we're anxious is to pray, and other times it's to pause and deal with what's going on in our bodies.

Yes, we are filled with the mighty, supernatural power of God—the same power that sent down fire from heaven and raised Jesus from the dead. But for now, that power dwells within a very human body. Sometimes the most spiritual thing we can do is have a snack and a glass of water, then take a nap.

God, I'm so grateful for your extraordinary compassion toward my humanity. Sometimes I'm so much harder on myself than you are. Help me be aware of not just what my soul needs but my body too. Thank you that every provision, whether spiritual or physical, is a gift from you. Amen.

God, you have made me both a physical and a spiritual being, so I ask that you bring *peace* to every part of my life—inner and outer. You are the one who brings *order* to my chaos, who brings *calm* to my heart. Amen.

God Never Lets You Battle Alone

"Don't be afraid!" Elisha told him. "For there are more on our side than on theirs!"

2 Kings 6:16

Startled by a noise, the prophet Elisha's servant wakes early and walks outside to investigate. Troops, horses, and chariots are everywhere. They've come to kill Elisha, and he won't be spared either. Turning to see Elisha behind him, he exclaims, "Oh, sir, what will we do now?" (2 Kings 6:15).

Confrontation is part of life, and one of the situations most likely to trigger our anxiety. Similar to the response of Elisha's servant, our initial reaction is likely to be fear or despair. When someone provokes our anxiety or attacks us, it can also be easy to lash out. Choosing to show kindness and calmness but not let ourselves get taken advantage of can be powerful.

We can remember there is a reality greater than what we see, rely on the truth that God has already given us spiritual victory, and respond with holy confidence. Anxiety tells us we have to handle everything on our own, but God promises we will never face any battle alone.

God, when I face confrontation, give me eyes to see beyond the human reality. Empower me to respond in faith rather than react in fear. Show me how to reflect both your strength and your love. Amen.

God Has You Here for Such a Time as This

> Who knows if perhaps you were made queen for just such a time as this?
>
> Esther 4:14

There's a myth that says a test of what God wants us to do is "having peace about it." That we won't experience fear or anxiety when doing what he wants. But Esther, Moses, and even Jesus in the garden of Gethsemane showed signs of human anxiety when they were right in the middle of God's plan for their lives.

Fear doesn't always mean turn back; sometimes it means move forward.

Faith doesn't mean never feeling anxious; it means obeying anyway.

You, too, are here for such a time as this.

God, you have placed me in this world for such a time as this. Open my eyes to what you're asking me to do each day. When the human part of me wants to settle for comfort and safety, give me the strength to be like Esther. Amen.

God Speaks to You in the Storm

Then the LORD spoke to Job out of the storm.

Job 38:1 NIV

Job thinks of all he has lost—his children, his possessions, and even his health. What will he do now? He sits for many days with his friends and processes all he's endured, including his questions, confusion, and frustration. His expressions of emotion include sorrow, rage, despair, and a desire for his life to end.

Finally, the Lord speaks to Job. He asks Job a series of questions like, "Where were you when I laid the earth's foundation?" (v. 4 NIV). At the end, Job says, "My ears had heard of you but now my eyes have seen you" (42:5 NIV). What Job needs most aren't answers to his questions but rather an assurance that God is real and he is still in control despite all that has happened.

If you have only been sharing with God what you think he wants to hear, then perhaps it's your turn to express what you truly feel and give God the opportunity to speak to you in the storm too.

God, you are so much bigger, wiser, and more compassionate than I can even comprehend. Give me the courage to bring all I feel to you, trusting you can take it. Amen.

God Is Your Good Shepherd

Even when I walk
    through the darkest valley,
I will not be afraid,
    for you are close beside me.
Your rod and your staff
    protect and comfort me.

Psalm 23:4

The shepherd's rod and staff provide protection from threats. Sheep are likely to get themselves into trouble, and so are we—especially when we're in a dark valley. But thankfully our Shepherd is always there to defend and rescue us.

Like David, we will go through dark valleys in life. No one experiences mountaintops all the time. But we can know that every time we descend into a valley, our Good Shepherd is with us. He will protect us with his rod, pursue us with his staff, and guide us to the other side.

God, you are my Good Shepherd, and I'm so grateful to be in your care. When I go through dark valleys, comfort me with your rod and staff. I trust you to get me through whatever I face. Amen.

God Sees the Desires of Your Heart

Take delight in the LORD,
    and he will give you your heart's desires.
Commit everything you do to the LORD.
    Trust him, and he will help you.

Psalm 37:4–5

One question it seems David anticipated the generations after him would ask is, "How do I know what God wants me to do?"

Very few times did God tell people *exactly* what to do, as he did with Moses parting the Red Sea. Most of the time he simply wanted people to have an intimate, lifelong relationship with him.

On the surface, David's words in Psalm 37 can sound like "delight in God and he'll do what you want." But the opposite is true. When we delight in God, our hearts are in sync with what *he* wants.

We don't have to be anxious about "getting it wrong." We can simply focus on loving God each day. This leads to more holy risking and less anxious retreating, more mistakes that help us learn and fewer missed opportunities, more pushing forward and less being paralyzed by fear.

When it's our turn to write "once I was young, and now I am old," as David did later in this same psalm (v. 25), we'll have stories worth passing on and hard-won wisdom to share too.

God, align my mind with yours. Align my heart with yours. Align my eyes, ears, mouth, hands, and feet with yours. Give me the courage to trust myself today because I trust in you. Amen.

God Gives You Rest

It is useless for you to work so hard
    from early morning until late at night,
anxiously working for food to eat;
    for God gives rest to his loved ones.

Psalm 127:2

The lie of anxiety is that something "out there" will give us the calm we crave. So we push ourselves, keep searching, try harder.

But this one phrase in Psalm 127:2 changes everything: "For God gives rest." This kind of rest isn't about a lack of physical activity. God encourages us to enjoy his good gifts, be productive, and take steps of obedience. Instead, this is about resting from anxiety-based striving that exhausts us and leaves us feeling empty.

Anxiety tells us having inner peace is about *what we can get.* The truth is, inner peace is *something only God can give.* What our souls truly need can't be bought or built; it can only be bestowed on us by a good God who invites us into grace.

God, give me the wisdom to know when anxiety is pushing me. Pull me back into your love and grace. You are the source of meaning in my life. You are the one who calms my heart and gives me rest. Amen.

God Soothes Your Soul

> I have calmed and quieted myself,
> like a weaned child who no longer
> cries for its mother's milk.
> Yes, like a weaned child is my soul
> within me.

Psalm 131:2

This verse from Psalms is a picture of contentment, not want; endearment, not distress; satisfaction, not seeking more.

A weaned child no longer connects with her mother from a place of need. It's not just about what the little one wants, it's about relationship. We can live like a weaned child by embracing spiritual practices like gratitude, praise, and reflection that aren't need-based but are simply about being with God.

Psalm 131 is dedicated to pilgrims journeying to Jerusalem. It was likely they would encounter challenges and anxiety-provoking situations along the way. We will too. But like a mother with her baby, God will be lovingly carrying us and caring for us.

God, I pause now to calm and quiet my soul before you. Thank you for carrying me every step of my journey. My soul is safe with you. Amen.

God Knows
Your Thoughts

Search me, O God, and know my heart;
test me and know my anxious thoughts.

Psalm 139:23

Research has shown that writing down our anxious thoughts can help. One way to do so is by creating a Worry Box. When you feel anxious about something, write it down on a piece of paper, then slide it into the Worry Box as a physical expression of giving it over to God. Every few months, open the box and write answered prayers on the back of the slips.

We're not going to shock, overwhelm, or disappoint God with what we share. Asking him to search us and know our anxious thoughts simply means we no longer have to face our anxiety alone. God will be there with us as our helper, guide, and faithful friend.

God, search me and know my heart;
test me and know my anxious thoughts.
Reveal to me the roots of my worries
and help me replace them with
truth. Thank you that I never have
to be alone in my anxiety. Amen.

God Is Greater Than All Your Fears

The fear of the LORD is the beginning
    of wisdom,
and knowledge of the Holy One is
    understanding.

Proverbs 9:10 NIV

Fearing God doesn't mean being scared of him. It means living in awe of who he is and all he has done. It means remembering he is bigger than everything, even our anxiety.

Anxiety is bossy. It tells us, "You can't go after that dream because you'll fail." It declares, "You have to be perfect or no one will love you." It threatens, "You must be on guard all the time or something terrible will happen." To silence it, we need to fear something more than its voice in our minds. Only God is big and powerful enough to fulfill that role.

We are to fear God, yet his "perfect love expels all fear" (1 John 4:18). It's a divine paradox; only by fearing God can we start overcoming our fear of everything else. He is our protector and provider, security and salvation, the soother of our souls and the mighty warrior who fights with love on our behalf anytime anxiety tries to bully us.

God, I fear you and approach you with awe, respect, humility, and trust. You are bigger than all my worries, more powerful than my anxiety, mightier than anything I will ever face. Amen.

God Alone Knows Your Future

You can make many plans,
  but the LORD's purpose will prevail.
                                    Proverbs 19:21

When making decisions, our brains naturally predict outcomes. But *we can never be completely sure of what we predict*. We're all just going through life making our best guesses about what will happen. God alone actually knows the future. That's why Proverbs 19:21 is so reassuring. It means that when we seek God, no matter what we choose, he will still accomplish his purpose in our lives.

God is able to get us where he wants us to go. He's able to redeem, redirect, and work all things together for our good. It's not up to us to get every detail of every decision perfect; our role is simply to depend on him and keep taking one small step after another. *Whew.*

God, you alone know my future and where you are leading me. Give me the courage to trust you, to keep moving forward one step at a time, believing your purposes in my life will prevail. Amen.

God Is in Your Everyday Moments

She is clothed with strength and dignity,
and she laughs without fear of the
future.

Proverbs 31:25

The Proverbs 31 woman uses a tactic those of us who struggle with anxiety can apply: She stays connected to the real world—what she can see, hear, touch, smell, and taste. Sometimes we dismiss these things as unspiritual, but they can actually be an essential part of managing our anxiety and being proactive.

When you're anxious, try pausing and noticing what you see, hear, taste, touch, and smell. Ground yourself in the present moment. Then take the next small action.

We tend to overspiritualize the Proverbs 31 woman, turning her into an ideal we can never attain. We do the same when it comes to dealing with our anxiety. We put pressure on ourselves to find huge and holy solutions. But as the Proverbs 31 woman knew, sometimes it's in the simple, ordinary moments of our lives that we experience God's extraordinary presence when we need it most.

God, when I get stuck in my head, reconnect me with the present moment, which is where you always are with me. Help me to see, touch, hear, smell, and taste your goodness all around me. Amen.

God Has a Time for Everything in Your Life

For everything there is a season,
   a time for every activity under heaven.

Ecclesiastes 3:1

Is it true that even anxiety has a season? Yes. If we smell smoke in our home, it's time to be anxious. Anxiety acts as an alarm system warning us of danger. It's essential to our physical survival and overall well-being.

But sometimes our anxiety alarm system goes off in unhelpful ways. A common example is when we worry about someone we love even though there's no reason to believe they're in harm's way and there's nothing we need to do to protect them. When our anxiety alarm system goes off, we can pause and ask ourselves two questions: "Is there a specific threat right now?" and "Do I need to take action right away?" If the answer is no, then it's likely un-helpful anxiety.

It's easy to tell ourselves we should *never* be anxious. But that's not realistic or even healthy. As wise Solomon knew, there really is a time for everything—even anxiety.

God, give me the wisdom to know when anxiety is helpful and when it's not. Give me the courage and self-discipline to bring all that concerns me to you. Amen.

God Is Not Done with Your Story

Don't be afraid, for I am with you.
  Don't be discouraged, for I am your God.
I will strengthen you and help you.
  I will hold you up with my victorious
    right hand.

Isaiah 41:10

God called Isaiah to speak his heart to his people during a difficult time in their history. No matter what happened, God would never stop loving them and calling them back to him. Isaiah reminds us of the one sure thing in our lives . . . *God himself.*

Isaiah is the book of the Bible with the most prophecies about the Messiah. In the middle of all that was happening, God's people could have hope because Jesus was coming. There will always be scary news headlines, wars, diseases, and everyday difficulties. In the middle of all that's *still* happening, we can have hope because Jesus is coming again.

Isaiah reminded God's people of what was true, and it's what we need to hear today too.

God is not done with history.

He's not done with your story either.

God, sometimes all that's going on in our world feels scary and overwhelming. You are my hope, and I choose to trust in you no matter what happens. When I'm tempted to let news headlines determine my day, help me remember that you alone get the final say. Amen.

God Gets You Through

When you go through deep waters,
   I will be with you.
When you go through rivers of difficulty,
   you will not drown.
When you walk through the fire of oppression,
   you will not be burned up;
   the flames will not consume you.

Isaiah 43:2

Noah and the ark, safe in the flood until dry land appeared again.

The people of Israel finally crossing the Jordan into the promised land after the wilderness.

Shadrach, Meshach, and Abednego thrown into the furnace and emerging untouched by the flames.

When the prophet Isaiah spoke the words in Isaiah 43:2, stories like these would have come to mind for God's people. And God is still writing stories of his faithfulness—showing up in our everyday lives, in the middle of our anxiety, reminding us that he is with us and for us.

Whatever we're facing, he's whispering encouragement to our hearts today too.

We are not alone in our deep waters.

We are not forsaken in our rivers of difficulty.

We are not abandoned to the flames.

No, we are God's people, and we are pressing on, refusing to give up, remembering we are loved in every circumstance. He will get us through.

God, you are the one with me in every difficult moment. I trust you will get me through whatever I face. You have never forsaken me, and you never will. Give me the strength I need today to persevere, and remind me you are here. Amen.

God Is Calling You

Don't be afraid of the people, for I will be with you and will protect you. I, the LORD, have spoken!

Jeremiah 1:8

God calls Jeremiah to be a prophet. But rather than replying with enthusiasm, Jeremiah protests, "O Sovereign LORD . . . I can't speak for you! I'm too young!" (v. 6). Like him, we're all tempted to believe the lie of anxiety that says we're "too" something.

Too young.

Too old.

Too quiet.

Too loud.

Too much.

Too little.

God addresses the real cause for Jeremiah's pause: "Don't be afraid of the people" (v. 8). When we say we're "too" something, usually we're worried about what people will think of us. Considering how others will view us is a natural and healthy part of being human. God created us to consider what people think of us; he just doesn't want us to be controlled by it. What he said to Jeremiah is true for us too: "I will be with you and will protect you."

God, when I feel anxious about what people think of me, support and protect me with your love. Give me the courage to listen to your voice, to believe you can use me, and to trust your plan for my future. Amen.

God Is Your Ultimate Certainty

Those who live at the ends of the earth
    stand in awe of your wonders.
From where the sun rises to where it sets,
    you inspire shouts of joy.

Psalm 65:8

When we're dealing with difficult circumstances or anxiety, we need security. When everything is changing, we need to know what will always be the same. In those moments, God himself says he will be our certainty.

To show us this is true, God has provided things we can count on in the world around us. Each sunrise reminds us his mercies are new every morning. Every sunset tells us that even as night comes, he is still in control. These rhythms in nature soothe us.

If you're in an anxiety-provoking season of life, rhythms and routines can create anchors for your soul. Going for an afternoon walk, journaling before bed at night, talking to a loved one each day, or taking a few minutes to pray can all be anchors. Notice what soothes and strengthens you, then repeat it.

In a changing world, we can count on a God of faithful love, of mercies that are new every morning . . . because that's how often we need them.

God, it's reassuring to know your faithful love never ends and your mercies are new every morning. Help me create rhythms in my life that reflect your consistency and care. Amen.

God Hears All
Your Prayers

Daniel answered, "Long live the king!
My God sent his angel to shut the lions'
mouths so that they would not hurt
me."

Daniel 6:21–22

Daniel surely felt some physical anxiety as he was thrown into the lions' den. But throughout all that happened he seemed to have a supernatural steadiness.

What was his secret? Part of it appeared to be his rhythm of praying three times a day. Whatever was going on his world, Daniel paused to pray. Like an elite athlete practicing, he trained himself to respond to anxiety-provoking situations with three steps: *pause, pray, repeat.*

We can try pausing, praying, and repeating whenever we begin to feel anxious. We can also explore a rhythm of prayer that fits our life as Daniel did.

Life is full of "lions' dens," and God will be with us in whatever situation we find ourselves in.

God, I'm grateful you invite me to connect with you anytime, anywhere, for any reason. Show me how to do so not just spontaneously but also consistently and intentionally. Help me train my heart, mind, and soul so that I'm ready for whatever comes. Amen.

God Brings New Life and Growth

Surely the LORD has done great things!
　　Don't be afraid, O land.
Be glad now and rejoice,
　　for the LORD has done great things.
Don't be afraid, you animals of the field,
　　for the wilderness pastures will
　　　soon be green.
The trees will again be filled with fruit;
　　fig trees and grapevines will be
　　　loaded down once more.

Joel 2:20–22

Scripture has a recurring theme of barren-ness followed by blessing, death followed by resurrection, loss followed by restoration. What can help us in those in-between times when life feels like it's on hold?

First, we can trust God is still working while we're waiting. Trust is not an emotion, it's a decision we make all over again each day. If you still struggle with challenging feelings, that's okay.

We can also look for even the smallest signs of new life and growth. Maybe you laughed hard for the first time in a while, or you sense a spark of creativity returning again.

In the best or worst of times, in celebration and sorrow, in laughter and languishing, in every season of change, who God is and his love for us remains the same.

God, it's a relief to know that even in the seasons when I feel weary, you are still working. Even when I'm waiting, you bring new life and growth to my soul. Amen.

God Gives You Truth for Temptation

Then Jesus was led by the Spirit into the wilderness to be tempted there by the devil.

Matthew 4:1

The temptation of Jesus is ultimately a battle between lies and truth. Those of us who struggle with anxiety need to know how to handle this kind of combat as well. Not all anxiety comes from lies, but we're more vulnerable to believing them when we're anxious.

Sometimes we can have the unrealistic expectation that as soon as we speak the truth, our anxiety will disappear. But Jesus had multiple rounds of combating lies before he won his battle in the wilderness. We're not spiritual failures if our anxiety doesn't go away after we quote one verse of Scripture. What matters is continuing to fight lies with truth until we experience victory. This might take minutes, days, weeks, or sometimes years.

We can take comfort in knowing that even Jesus, the Son of God, was tempted to believe lies. He understands what it's like, and he will empower us to live in the truth.

God, you are the one who helps me have victory. Show me the lies I've believed and set me free with your truth. Amen.

God Is Your Caretaker

> That is why I tell you not to worry about everyday life—whether you have enough food and drink, or enough clothes to wear. Isn't life more than food, and your body more than clothing?
>
> Matthew 6:25

Worry differs from anxiety in that it's specific and usually about something in our external circumstances. Jesus addresses this in his Sermon on the Mount when he tells his listeners not to worry about everyday material needs like food and clothes.

As an antidote for worry, Jesus tells the crowd to look at the birds and how God feeds them, at the lilies and how God dresses them (see vv. 26, 28). By doing so, Jesus reminds us of God's care.

It's spring here, and I just opened my window. A robin is building a nest in a tree. Wildflowers are blooming around the little pond behind our house. They don't seem worried or hurried, stressed-out or weary. God is taking good care of them today, and he promises to do the same for us too.

God, thank you for taking care of the birds, the flowers, and me. When my mind tries to wander into worry, bring it back to the present—the place where you are with me right now, providing my every need. Amen.

God Invites You to Rest

> Then Jesus said, "Come to me, all of you who are weary and carry heavy burdens, and I will give you rest. Take my yoke upon you. Let me teach you, because I am humble and gentle at heart, and you will find rest for your souls. For my yoke is easy to bear, and the burden I give you is light."
>
> Matthew 11:28–30

When someone shares a "should" that makes us feel heavy, as if we're being handed a burden, we need to beware. Jesus says about the Pharisees, "They crush people with unbearable religious demands and never lift a finger to ease the burden" (Matt. 23:4).

In contrast to the Pharisees, Jesus says, "I am humble and gentle at heart, and you will find rest for your souls. For my yoke is easy to bear, and the burden I give you is light" (11:29–30).

Instead of striving, he invites us to rest. Instead of being perfect, he offers us freedom and forgiveness. Instead of making life about performance, he brings us into perfect love.

Learning from others can be helpful, and we live in a time with an extraordinary amount of information. That is a gift, but we also need to be aware of when it starts being a source of anxiety and guilt.

We don't need more shoulds; we need more grace.

God, thank you for being the ultimate source of truth and grace. When I place "shoulds" on my shoulders, help me choose the lightness and freedom you offer instead. Amen.

God Is Your Supplier and Multiplier

> Then he took the seven loaves and the fish, thanked God for them, and broke them into pieces. He gave them to the disciples, who distributed the food to the crowd.
>
> Matthew 15:36

In the moments when we feel "not enough," the story of Jesus feeding the four thousand from Matthew 15:32–39 offers us hope and help. First, it reassures us that we can offer God what we have, even if it feels like very little. In his hands, there is no such thing as "small."

We also don't have to be the ultimate source of what others need; we're only to pass on what we've already received.

God says nothing is impossible with him. God reminds us all we really need is to trust him. God promises to be not only our supplier but also our multiplier.

God, anxiety tries to tell me I'm limited by my human capabilities. But you tell me that with you, nothing is impossible for me. You are my strength when I'm weak. You are my supplier when the needs seem like too much. You are the Savior who still empowers me to serve others. Amen.

God Lets You Draw Near

Then the frightened woman, trembling at the realization of what had happened to her, came and fell to her knees in front of him and told him what she had done. And he said to her, "Daughter, your faith has made you well. Go in peace. Your suffering is over."

Mark 5:33–34

Our anxiety can make us feel like this woman. It tells us, *You shouldn't be here. You shouldn't do this. It's too late for you.* It can go on for years. We may visit many doctors, try many cures. Religious people might rebuke us, make us feel "less than" in our faith. Perhaps we even worry God is mad at us. Can we touch the edge of Jesus's robe too?

Yes. We have a God who is approachable. We're invited to do more than just touch the edge of his robe. We have full access to his presence and power whenever we need it.

Anxiety will lie to us and say God wants us only once we're whole. But the truth is, we can come to him anytime we need to, in whatever condition we're in, knowing his response will always be one of love, grace, and understanding.

We are not strangers in a crowd to God. We are his beloved daughters and sons.

God, thank you for seeing the suffering anxiety causes in my life and responding not with a rebuke but with great care and affection. I'm reaching out to you today. Amen.

God Calms Your Heart

> When Jesus woke up, he rebuked the wind and the raging waves. Suddenly the storm stopped and all was calm.
>
> Luke 8:24

This miracle of calming the storm happens fairly early in Jesus's ministry. The disciples have been called by him, have listened to his teachings, and have even seen him perform miracles. But they've not yet answered with absolute certainty this crucial question: "Is Jesus really, truly God in every moment of my life?"

It's the question we ask ourselves when the storms of life come. Anxiety will tell us the answer is no. The boat is sinking, and we're in charge of saving ourselves. But the true answer is yes, Jesus is God no matter the circumstances or how we may feel. He is always with us and for us.

The disciples experienced the complete calming of a physical storm. This side of heaven, the emotional storms we're in may not fully go away. Sometimes the storms calm, and sometimes we find calm in the storm because we know with certainty these two things: God is God in every moment of our lives, and with him, we can make it through anything.

God, when storms come, I pray for your supernatural calm, either by causing the storm to cease or by giving me hope, strength, and inner stillness in the middle of it. You are God in every moment of my life. Amen.

God Invites You to Stop Striving

But the Lord said to her, "My dear Martha, you are worried and upset over all these details! There is only one thing worth being concerned about. Mary has discovered it, and it will not be taken away from her."

Luke 10:41–42

Jesus knows how hard Martha has tried. He sees the weight of responsibility that's so heavy on her shoulders. His words could have felt like a rebuke, but instead they're more like a long-overdue release.

Anxiety tells all of us, but especially those of us who took on a lot of responsibility in childhood, "You can have control." We want our loved ones safe, the dinner to be perfect, and everything to turn out the way we'd hope.

But life is unpredictable. What we need more than control is to know that someone else is in charge of everything, that he is good and he loves us. What we really need—the "one thing worth being concerned about"—is intimacy with Someone who will take care of us no matter what happens.

God, you've been with me every moment of my life. You know the responsibilities I may have taken on that you never intended for me. When they cause me to strive and stress out, please reveal the true source of my anxiety and set me free. Amen.

God Knows How It Feels

He took Peter and . . . James and John, and he became anguished and distressed. He told them, "My soul is crushed with grief to the point of death. Stay here and keep watch with me."

Matthew 26:37–38

When Jesus was betrayed, arrested, falsely accused, and forced to carry his cross, a supernatural peace sustained him. Yet his body still responded to what was happening. Jesus was so distressed in Gethsemane that Luke, a disciple and doctor, wrote in his Gospel that Jesus even experienced hematohidrosis (sweating blood).

In times of stress, you may experience physical symptoms too. This doesn't mean your faith is weak or you're doing something wrong. You're not in trouble with God for how your body is responding. It doesn't mean you're spiritually failing; it means you're a human doing hard, courageous things.

And Jesus knows exactly what that feels like.

God, thank you for coming to earth and taking on a physical body like ours. It's such a relief and gift to know you understand how hard being human is sometimes. I trust you with all of who I am—spiritual, emotional, and physical. Amen.

God Can Heal
in Many Ways

Jesus told him, "Stand up, pick up your mat, and walk!"

John 5:8

We serve a God who is limitless, who heals in so many different ways. He uses wise counselors, gifted doctors, caring friends and family. He has given us prayer, his Word, and his love. He also provides practical tools.

Sometimes we're told God can use miracles but not medicine; preachers but not doctors; Scripture but not a good night's sleep. But "whatever is good and perfect is a gift coming down to us from God our Father" (James 1:17).

Before the man at the pool of Bethesda picked up his mat and walked, Jesus asked him, "Would you like to get well?" Perhaps we're tempted to respond to that question the same way the man did at first: "I can't" (John 5:6–7).

But we can choose to believe more is possible than we may have imagined. We can say, "Yes, Jesus, show me how you want to heal me. I believe you know what I need most today."

God, you are a limitless healer, and I open myself up to whoever and whatever you want to use to help my anxiety. You care about every part of who I am—heart, soul, mind, and body. I entrust all of me to you. Amen.

God Frees You from Fear

The jailer called for lights and ran to the dungeon and fell down trembling before Paul and Silas. Then he brought them out and asked, "Sirs, what must I do to be saved?"

Acts 16:29–30

The jailer in this story discovers fear can have interesting side effects. It reminds us of our need for God. It keeps us humble. It shows us that we are small. It lets us see our inadequacy. It reveals the temporary nature of all that surrounds us.

All of this is exceedingly uncomfortable. But it can also be a neon arrow pointing us to the one who loves us. Fear is not from God, but he can use it to draw us closer to him.

Paul and Silas told the jailer all he needed to do was believe in Jesus, and he joyfully did so. At midnight he thought his life was over, but by dawn he had brought Paul and Silas "into his house and set a meal before them, and he and his entire household rejoiced because they all believed in God" (v. 34).

From fear to faith.

From thinking life is over to beginning a new one.

From isolation to celebration.

From prison to new freedom.

God changes everything.

God, you are the one who sets my heart free from fear. When I'm afraid, help me see that fear as a reminder to reach out to you for help. Amen.

God's Love Is Given, Not Earned

And I am convinced that nothing can ever separate us from God's love. Neither death nor life, neither angels nor demons, neither our fears for today nor our worries about tomorrow—not even the powers of hell can separate us from God's love.

Romans 8:38

When anxiety tries to tell you God's love is conditional or you must earn his approval, cling to this truth: Nothing can separate you from God's love—no exceptions. No mistake or shortcoming, no weakness or struggle, no relapse or rule broken. Not even that secret you've never told anyone. Not that battle you lost again yesterday. Not the critical voice in your mind.

You never have to ask, "What can I do to earn God's approval?" because his love is a gift and his grace is a certainty you can count on for all eternity.

God, thank you that nothing can ever separate me from your love. When my anxiety tries to tell me that's not true, draw me back to your grace. Amen.

God Renews Your Mind

> Don't copy the behavior and customs of this world, but let God transform you into a new person by changing the way you think. Then you will learn to know God's will for you, which is good and pleasing and perfect.
>
> Romans 12:2

If we live in a culture motivated by fear, then changing the way we think means learning to be motivated instead by faith.

One way we can do this is by noticing how the news we consume affects us. Does what we're reading, watching, or hearing cause us to experience fear? Even if it is true, where will we put our trust—in newsmakers or in the Maker of heaven and earth?

As we change how we think, the way Paul encourages us to do in this verse, our brains actually make new pathways. True transformation takes persistence and perseverance.

When you feel anxiety rising and want to turn on the TV or reach for your phone to check just one more headline, pause, take a deep breath, and say, "Not this time, fear. With God's help, I'm renewing my mind."

God, you know everything that has ever happened in this world and my life. Help me consume news in ways that lead to more peace in my heart instead of having the news consume me. Amen.

God Doesn't Need You to Be Perfect

> I came to you in weakness—timid and trembling. And my message and my preaching were very plain. Rather than using clever and persuasive speeches, I relied only on the power of the Holy Spirit. I did this so you would trust not in human wisdom but in the power of God.
>
> 1 Corinthians 2:3–5

We're not used to hearing about weakness from modern spiritual leaders. In our world, high energy, a big personality, and smooth delivery are often the expectations. Because of that, we believe this lie: *If my anxiety shows, God can't use me.*

But in these verses Paul says that our weakness can point people to the power of God. He may also have come "timid and trembling" for another reason: Paul wanted the Corinthians to trust him. Before becoming a believer, he persecuted, threatened, and was eager to kill Christians.

The Corinthians didn't need to see Paul give a perfect performance. They needed to see he had been transformed by Jesus. It's okay if sometimes our anxiety shows. Those might unexpectedly be the moments when God shows most in us too.

God, thank you that I don't have to be perfect for you to use me. I can even be timid and trembling. Give me the courage not to hold back until I have it all together but to show up as I am—to you be all the glory. Amen.

God Clears the Clutter in Your Life

> For God is not a God of disorder but of peace.
>
> 1 Corinthians 14:33

We often think of clutter only in terms of extra items in our home, but it takes multiple forms.

We can experience sound clutter because of all the sound notifications we receive through our phones. There's also visual clutter, like when our house is always messy or the stacks of paper on our desk drive us crazy. We can also have time clutter, which happens when our schedules become too full. Financial clutter means we have extra expenses that consume resources but don't add to the quality of our lives. Emotional clutter happens when we collect hurts but never take time to deal with them.

When we're feeling anxious and can't understand why, one of the most helpful questions we can ask ourselves is, "Where do I have clutter in my life?" Once we identify the source, we can start bringing order to that area again.

Our nervous system can only handle so much before we start feeling anxious, and learning what leads to peace in our lives can be part of healing.

God, reveal any clutter in my life that's causing my anxiety. Then show me what I need to let go of so I can be free and live with greater peace today. Amen.

God Is Strong
in Our Weakness

Three different times I begged the Lord to take it away. Each time he said, "My grace is all you need. My power works best in weakness." So now I am glad to boast about my weaknesses, so that the power of Christ can work through me.

2 Corinthians 12:8–9

The apostle Paul never shares specifics about the "thorn" in his flesh that he begs God to take away. But those of us who struggle with anxiety can relate to having something in our lives we wish would disappear completely. I've asked God many times to free me fully from my anxiety, but that hasn't happened yet.

God created each of us in an amazing and wonderful way. Because we live in a fallen world, we each have potential struggles and powerful strengths. Yes, anxiety can feel like a thorn in our flesh. But sometimes thorns come with beautiful things. For example, research shows people who struggle with anxiety also often have high empathy. As a quote often attributed to author Henry Van Dyke says, "The best rose-bush, after all, is not that which has the fewest thorns, but that which bears the finest roses."

God, I choose to believe you made me in an amazing and wonderful way, even if I don't always feel like it. Help me embrace who I am and become all you've created me to be a little more each day. Amen.

God Overpowers Perfectionism

So Christ has truly set us free. Now make sure that you stay free, and don't get tied up again in slavery to the law.

Galatians 5:1

Our personal version of the law is usually whatever we're trusting in to gain approval and affection. Sometimes the laws we follow come from authority figures in our childhood. *Thou shall never make the family look bad.* Sometimes they come from religious organizations. *Thou shall be at church every time the doors are open.* We can pick them up from the culture around us. *Thou shall never age.* Or we might go through trauma that makes them seem necessary for our survival. *Thou shall not trust anyone ever again.* Our anxiety throws laws at us all the time. *Thou shall never mess up in public.*

God doesn't condemn us for these laws. Quite the opposite, he's still in the business of setting people pleasers and perfectionists free.

Because of Jesus, we no longer have to earn approval, hustle for love, prove our worth, or try to be good enough for God. We are no longer under any law; we are under grace. Perfectionism and pressure have lost their power over us. "Christ has truly set us free."

God, thank you for setting me free from fear, perfectionism, and living under the law. Help me fully embrace your grace. Amen.

God Gives You Armor for Anxiety

Be strong in the Lord and in his mighty power. Put on the full armor of God, so that you can take your stand against the devil's schemes.

Ephesians 6:10–11 NIV

Most of us have heard of the armor of God, but how can we use it in our battle with anxiety?

When we start to feel anxious, one strategy we can try is to picture ourselves putting on the armor of God one piece at a time from head to toe, praying as we do so.

The belt of truth defends against the lies of anxiety.

The breastplate of righteousness guards our hearts.

The shoes of the gospel of peace help us stand firm.

The shield of faith protects us from the enemy's attacks.

The helmet of salvation covers our minds.

The sword of the Spirit empowers us to fight back.

We're in an invisible battle, but we serve an invincible God—and with him we are mightier than we know.

God, thank you for giving me the armor I need to fight my battles. With you, I am not a worrier but a warrior, and anxiety will not win. Amen.

God Will Help You Fight for Peace

Don't worry about anything; instead, pray about everything. Tell God what you need, and thank him for all he has done. Then you will experience God's peace, which exceeds anything we can understand.

Philippians 4:6–7

It's easy to think peace is something that will simply descend on us the first time we ask for God's help. But in my experience, it's something we fight for over and over. Thankfully, Paul gives us a battle plan.

Don't worry about anything.

Pray about everything.

Tell God what you need.

Thank him for all he has done.

Repeat, repeat, repeat.

Is this easy? Absolutely not. Will there be times when we *do* worry, even feel despair? Yes, we are human, after all. Will we experience resistance? Every day.

But we are not alone in the fight. And, over time, the battle will get less intense.

If you have to fight for peace, nothing is wrong with your faith. There is peace that comes from the absence of all pain or difficulty. But there is a deeper, more powerful peace that comes after the heat of battle. This is the kind of peace only warriors know.

Fight on.

God, when peace requires a battle, give me the strength to fight. I'm so glad to know you're with me and you will guard my heart and mind. Amen.

God Retrains Your Brain

Fix your thoughts on what is true, and honorable, and right, and pure, and lovely, and admirable. Think about things that are excellent and worthy of praise.

Philippians 4:8

"Fix your thoughts . . ." When the apostle Paul wrote these words, he didn't mean to repair what's broken. Instead, *fix* here means to focus our thoughts in a consistent, intentional way. This is like a mental workout, and it takes repetition and persistence.

Here's an exercise that helps me: Every morning I spend a few minutes visualizing a room full of people I love. I walk around and give each one a hug. Sometimes I picture Jesus in the room too. I engage all my senses—what do I see, hear, smell, touch, even taste? The more details I can add, the more my brain will engage. This exercise reminds me that everything I do that day is really about loving God, others, and myself. It helps me live from a place of belonging and grace, which also significantly decreases my anxiety.

Ask God for scenes that will realign your thoughts, calm your mind, and draw you closer to him. *What we focus on, we will go toward in life*. We can drift into negativity or intentionally redirect our thoughts to what is life-giving, heart-freeing, and true.

God, you have given me a powerful mind. Help me focus on what is true, honorable, right, pure, lovely, excellent, and worthy of praise today. Amen.

God Equips You to Handle Anything

I have learned to be content whatever the circumstances. I know what it is to be in need, and I know what it is to have plenty. I have learned the secret of being content in any and every situation, whether well fed or hungry, whether living in plenty or in want. I can do all this through him who gives me strength.

Philippians 4:11–13 NIV

Paul says he has *learned* to be content. That's a relief because it means contentment is a skill, not an emotion. Knowing that can take the pressure off us to make ourselves feel a certain way.

Like all skills, living with contentment takes practice. In the original language, one meaning of *content* is "independent of external circumstances."[1] When we're anxious, external circumstances (or our thoughts about them) can control us. So practicing contentment means taking back that control.

How can we do so? Paul's secret gives us an answer. We can pause and say like he did, "With Jesus, I can handle whatever happens." Then we can refocus on the present rather than get distracted by a fear-filled future that may never come to be.

Think back over your life and the difficulties you've already overcome. If someone had told you in advance about those, you might have said, "If that happens, I won't be able to handle it." But you had the strength you needed because God gave it to you. You've handled hard times before, and when new challenges arise, you can be confident you'll do so again with Jesus's help.

God, no matter what happens, you and I will handle it together. Thank you that nothing is too much for me because you will always give me the strength I need. Amen.

God Can Even Use Conflict

Is there any encouragement from belonging to Christ? Any comfort from his love? Any fellowship together in the Spirit? Are your hearts tender and compassionate? Then make me truly happy by agreeing wholeheartedly with each other, loving one another, and working together with one mind and purpose.

Philippians 2:1–2

The apostle Paul expresses concern for two kinds of peace in the lives of the Philippians: peace *within* each of them and peace *between* them in their relationships. Conflict is one of the most anxiety-provoking situations, and it's nothing new.

To help us take the anxiety that conflict stirs up and replace it with peace, one of the first steps can be getting rid of lies we've believed about conflict.

Lie: All conflict is bad.

Truth: Conflict is sometimes a necessary part of healthy relationships.

Lie: God wants me to get along with everyone all the time.

Truth: Jesus himself didn't get along with everyone all the time.

Lie: I can't handle anyone being mad at me.

Truth: Someone being mad at me is uncomfortable but not unbearable.

When we start engaging in healthy conflict instead of avoiding it, our anxiety may increase in the short term. But as issues involving other people in our lives get resolved, we may discover we experience more peace in the long term. Healthy conflict can cause anxiety, but sometimes it's also the best way to cure it.

God, give me wisdom about when and how to engage in healthy conflict. Bring a new level of true peace to my heart and relationships. Amen.

God Connects with You in Creative Ways

> Since you have been raised to new life with Christ, set your sights on the realities of heaven, where Christ sits in the place of honor at God's right hand. Think about the things of heaven, not the things of earth.
>
> Colossians 3:1–2

When Paul wrote to the Colossians, he'd not yet visited their church. He'd only heard reports that false teachers were trying to persuade new believers to go down a destructive path. Paul wrote as a protective spiritual father and mentor, reminding the Colossians to keep their faith and focus.

Anxiety can be like a "false teacher" in our lives. It tells us lies, like we're not good enough, we have to try harder, or no one will love us unless we're perfect. When that happens, it can help if we intentionally stop listening to the voice of anxiety and start returning to truth.

What's one small way you can do that today? It might be going for a walk and thinking about a particular verse, word, or phrase from Scripture that helps calm you. It could mean reaching out to a wise, truth-speaking friend. You may start your day by reading the Bible as you have your morning coffee.

Whatever helps you hear God's voice of love and grace above all others can help you quiet the voice of anxiety too.

God, I love that there are so many ways I can connect with you. When anxiety tries to be a "false teacher" in my life and take me down a destructive path, lead me toward you instead in creative ways. Amen.

God, you never put pressure on me. Instead, you set me free. When I start taking on *goals* you never intended, help me trade them for your *grace*. Amen.

God Is the Ultimate Trainer

> Physical training is good, but training for godliness is much better, promising benefits in this life and in the life to come.
>
> 1 Timothy 4:8

We likely know how to exercise our bodies, but how do we exercise our spiritual lives, as Paul encourages Timothy to do in this verse?

One simple way is meditation. Some of us have been taught that *meditate* is a scary word, but it actually just means intentionally thinking deeply or focusing. The Psalms give us three areas that can work well for meditation:

- *God's love.* "We meditate on your unfailing love" (48:9).
- *God's ways and truth.* "I will meditate on your decrees" (119:23).

- *God's character and power.* "I will meditate on your majestic, glorious splendor and your wonderful miracles" (145:5).

Try finding a quiet place, setting a timer for five minutes, and intentionally thinking about one of those three themes. It's okay if you get distracted. That's normal, and each time you refocus your thoughts you're strengthening your heart, soul, and mind.

God, you've made my body, heart, soul, and mind in amazing ways. Help me to use every part of who I am to love you, others, and myself today. Amen.

God Has Not Given You a Spirit of Fear

> For God has not given us a spirit of fear and timidity, but of power, love, and self-discipline.
>
> 2 Timothy 1:7

The temptation when we hear the words *power*, *love*, and *self-discipline* is to make them a personal checklist we have to accomplish on our own. When anxiety strikes, we tell ourselves to stop being afraid, get over it, push through, slap on a smile, and pretend we're fine. But we don't have to fake or force anything. We've been given a Spirit who lives within us and empowers us. We can take Paul's words to Timothy and turn them into an affirmation to repeat in anxious moments: "God has not given me a spirit of fear and timidity, but of power, love, and self-discipline."

Saying these words doesn't mean our fear will magically go away. But it will remind us that we, like Timothy, have everything we need to move forward in faith and finish strong.

God, thank you for giving me a spirit not of fear but of power, love, and self-discipline. I pray that you will empower me through your Spirit today. Amen.

God Empowers You to Run Your Race

> Therefore, since we are surrounded by such a huge crowd of witnesses to the life of faith, let us strip off every weight that slows us down, especially the sin that so easily trips us up. And let us run with endurance the race God has set before us.
>
> Hebrews 12:1

Negative, high-intensity emotions like anxiety are *heavy*. When we experience anxiety, we can intentionally set down what's weighing on us and return to calm with the help of Jesus.

For example, if I find myself caught up in worry, I can first notice that I've taken on extra weight. I can pause and pray, "Jesus, please help me give this to you." Then I can pursue calm by taking a few deep breaths, going for a walk, or reaching out to a friend. I may need to repeat this many times a day, and that's okay.

Ancient runners knew what our anxious hearts need to understand too. The ultimate goal of a race is progress, not perfection. It's perseverance, not a flawless performance. It's simply moving toward the finish line one step at a time.

God, you are the one who empowers me to run the race you have for me. Help me lay down anything that hinders me, like fear and anxiety. I will keep taking one step at a time toward the finish line. Amen.

God Gets You Through Stress to Joy

> Consider it pure joy, my brothers and sisters, whenever you face trials of many kinds.
>
> James 1:2 NIV

True confession: I don't like this verse, but lately I've been starting to think James is onto something. When psychologist and author Kelly McGonigal did in-depth research on stress, she reached a similar conclusion. She writes, "When it came to overall well-being, the happiest people in the poll weren't the ones without stress. . . . I call this the *stress paradox*. High levels of stress are associated with both distress and well-being."[1]

When we struggle with anxiety, it can be easy to assume the answer is to make our lives stress-free. But if we eliminate everything that ever causes us any stress, it could actually mean the absence of things we long for—like relationships and growth.

Stress is uncomfortable, and we don't ever have to like it. But it can be helpful to know our lives don't have to be stress-free for us to experience joy. In ways beyond what we may understand, it's not either/or but both/and.

God, when life feels stressful, show me the hidden joy and meaning. Thank you for redeeming everything in my life, even stress, and using it all for my best. Amen.

God Transforms Being Anxious

You will be anxious to do the will of God.

1 Peter 4:2

Does it surprise you to see *anxious* used in a positive way in Scripture? It's easy to think of our anxiety as "all bad," but research has found it's actually closely related to another emotion—excitement. When we're told to be anxious to do the will of God, it means we're to be excited to do the will of God.

"Anxiety and excitement are both aroused emotions. In both, the heart beats faster, cortisol surges, and the body prepares for action.... The only difference is that excitement is a positive emotion, focused on all the ways something could go well."[1] Anxiety and calm are opposites; anxiety and excitement are cousins.

One technique that can help us shift from anxiety to excitement is asking ourselves, "What do I really want?" An Olympic athlete is a good example of this. Anxiety for them sounds like, "I don't want to fail." Excitement sounds like, "I want to do my absolute best."

When we try to shift from anxiety to excitement, it might feel forced or fake—especially in the beginning. It's okay to have a good laugh about how awkward it sometimes feels to do this, and it may take a few tries before it works. If this feels impossible for you right now, that's okay too.

Sometimes we can eliminate our anxiety.

Sometimes we can transform it into something new.

God, when I'm anxious in a fear-based way, help me shift my perspective. I am anxious to do your will, and I'm trusting you to empower me to do so today. Amen.

God Lets You Cast Your Cares on Him

Cast all your anxiety on him because he cares for you.

1 Peter 5:7 NIV

Sometimes we put pressure on ourselves to just "cast our cares on God" and then feel like spiritual failures when our worries come back again. But Peter, a fisherman, would have known casting is repetitive. He didn't just cast his net once; he did it over and over again. We may need to do the same.

Releasing our cares isn't a onetime event. It's a lifelong process. We can come to the shore of God's faithful love as often as we need. Yes, we are always welcome to give him whatever weighs us down so that we can continue our journey with freer, lighter hearts.

To cast our cares means more than just a tentative letting go—it's a hurling, tossing, complete release. This is the offer of God: to let him take our anxieties fully and completely as often as we need.

God, I'm grateful for the invitation to cast my cares on you. None of them are too big or too small. Help me release them all to you. Amen.

God's Love for You Is Perfect

See how very much our Father loves us,
for he calls us his children, and that is
what we are!

1 John 3:1

When we're anxious, we can ask ourselves,
"What's one thing I can do that will help
me know and rely on God's love for me?" We
might tell a trustworthy friend or counselor
we're not okay and let them speak encouragement to us. We may go for a walk in nature so
we can see how God cares for the birds, the
flowers, and us. We could pause to pray, listen
to music that calms us, or embrace the gift
of rest through a much-needed nap. What we
choose doesn't have to be "religious"—it only
needs to reveal more of God's love in our lives.

The apostle John discovered a heart-freeing
truth we can embrace today. Even in our anxious

moments, two things never change: God's love and our true identity. We are fully and always beloved.

God, help me know and rely on the love you have for me today. Open my eyes to see your love everywhere. Open my ears to hear it wherever I go. Open my hands and heart to fully receive it. I want to live as your beloved. Amen.

God Loves You Without Judgment

> There is no judgment against anyone
> who believes in him.
>
> John 3:18

When we get to heaven, it will be a joyful homecoming. We'll have crossed the finish line and the great cloud of witnesses can cheer. We'll see Jesus face-to-face at last.

On the cross when he took God's wrath for us, when he died for our sins, Jesus said, "It is finished" (John 19:30). There is no eternal "PS" to that statement. There's not an "oops, I forgot that one really terrible thing you did." We are right with God today. We are right with God tomorrow. We are right with God for all eternity.

The story that will be told when we get to heaven will be one of victory. It will be about all Jesus has done for us. It will be about grace and love far beyond what we can even imagine.

God, thank you that because I've trusted in Jesus as my Savior, I can be absolutely at peace about standing before you one day. I so look forward to that time, and I thank you that your grace will sustain me until I get there. I'm so grateful for your love and faithfulness. Amen.

God Is with You in Every Stressful Moment

God replied to Moses, "I AM WHO I AM. Say this to the people of Israel: I AM has sent me to you."

Exodus 3:14

We can take comfort in knowing God is with us even in our hard places. Our challenges do not change his character or commitment.

Paul writes in Romans 8:38, "I am convinced that nothing can ever separate us from God's love. Neither death nor life, neither angels nor demons, neither our fears for today nor our worries about tomorrow—not even the powers of hell can separate us from God's love."

Here's what we all need to know in every stress-ful moment:

God is with me right now.

God is with *you* right now.

And whatever tomorrow brings, he will be there too.

God, thank you for always being with me. You are present in every stressful moment, and you alone can bring me the peace I need. I'm so grateful nothing can separate me from your love. Help me trust you with everything that brings me stress, whether big or small, knowing you care about it all. Amen.

God Gives You Less Stress, More Peace

Peace be with you, dear brothers and sisters.

Ephesians 6:23

Understanding stress matters, because stressed-out people often experience guilt or shame about the way they feel. Or they become determined to get rid of stress completely. But what we really need is to know how to make stress work for us, to keep it from wearing us out and bossing us around.

Think of your natural stress response like a wild horse. It can trample your yard and throw you onto the dirt. But it can also be tamed. And when that happens, it has surprising potential to help you move forward in life. What makes the difference? *Who's in control.* God will help you show your stress who's boss.

God, you know every detail of my life. You know the pressures I have, the challenges I face, and the moments when I grow tired and weary. You don't condemn me for experiencing stress; instead, you come alongside me to lead me back toward peace. Guide me on this journey. I give all that concerns me to you. Amen.

God Gives You a Better Response

Instead, let the Spirit renew your thoughts and attitudes. Put on your new nature, created to be like God—truly righteous and holy.

Ephesians 4:23–24

The fight-or-flight response is necessary for our survival. But our brains have two other responses to stress that can prove much more helpful.

The first is the challenge response. Think of a time when you were afraid but also determined to take action. In the challenge response, we tell ourselves, "I've got this" or, as believers, "I've got this because God's got me."

The second is called tend-and-befriend. Asking, "Who can I help right now?" helps shift our brains out of fight-or-flight mode.

We all experience the fight-or-flight response, especially when the unexpected happens, but we don't have to stay in it. God said he'll take care of the birds and flowers I see outside my window. He also takes care of us in many ways—including giving us remarkable, adaptable brains.

God, thank you for giving me a brain that can respond and adapt in many ways to whatever happens. When I feel stuck in fear, help me see it as a challenge that you and I can handle together so I can take action. And give me the courage to help others, because we are better and braver together. Amen.

God Brings You True Peace

The LORD gives his people strength.
The LORD blesses them with peace.

Psalm 29:11

In our culture, we tend to think of peace as the absence of what troubles us. The biblical word for peace is *Shalom*, which essentially means wholeness and well-being. Theologian Tim Keller says, "Shalom experienced is multidimensional, complete well-being—physical, psychological, social, and spiritual; it flows from all of one's relationships being put right—with God, within oneself, and with others."[1]

If we're in a season where life is hard and stressful, then that means we let Shalom be our hope. True peace isn't just the absence of something; it is the presence of Someone. A God who loves us. A God who is for us. A God who is making all things new, including me and you.

God, you don't just give me peace; you are my peace. Thank you that what you offer is so much deeper and greater than I often know. I ask that you give me Shalom so that no matter what my circumstances might be, I can know that all will be well and I will be whole. Amen.

God Can Shift Your Perspective

For as he thinks in his heart, so is he.

Proverbs 23:7 NKJV

Psychologist Martin Seligman suggests there are two distinct ways of explaining events in our lives: pessimism and optimism. Pessimism means we see unfortunate events as being our fault, lasting forever, and affecting every area of our lives. Optimism means we see those same events as being caused by something outside ourselves, not lasting forever, and only being related to a specific situation.[1]

Explaining events to ourselves in a more optimistic rather than pessimistic way can help us be resilient. It also minimizes the long-term damage to our emotional, mental, and physical health as well as to our relationships. And while Seligman calls this optimism, it sure feels a lot to me like living in grace. As believers, we aren't limited to just "pessimist" or "optimist." We can go above and beyond those labels because we're indwelled by and empowered through the Spirit.

We often can't control what happens to us. But we can control what we think about it. And that can make all the difference.

God, you have given me a powerful mind that shapes how I view myself and my circumstances. When I start to give in to negativity and self-criticism, shift me back toward grace and compassion. I so often do this for others, but it's much harder to do for myself. Empower me to do so today. Amen.

God Provides Satisfaction for Your Soul

He lets me rest in green meadows;
  he leads me beside peaceful streams.

Psalm 23:2

The metaphor in Psalm 23 is of a shepherd and sheep. A modern-day sheep rancher says, "Sheep prefer to drink still water as opposed to water from a moving stream."[1] It seems it's easier for humans and sheep to receive what they need when there's not a rush.

We may think we have to settle for a quick sip, that God's priority is for us to cover as much ground as we can in as little time as we can. But his true invitation is for us to slow down, drink deep, and take all the time we need.

This is the miracle and mystery: God is pointing us not to an external source to meet our needs but to *himself*. He himself is the water, the one we thirst for with all our being.

God, you know how easy it is for humans to get caught up in moving fast and going far. In every moment, whether I'm busy or being still, help me remember that when my heart is weary and my soul is thirsty, I can come to you. You offer me what I most need to receive, what I can't get anywhere else. Amen.

God Gives You Breath

A peaceful heart leads to a healthy body.
Proverbs 14:30

We experience anxiety when our fight-or-flight system is triggered. To return to a more peaceful state, our bodies need to turn off that system again. One technique that seems to work well for me is box breathing.

Let's try it together . . .

Sitting upright, breathe in through your nose for a count of four until your lungs are full.

Hold that breath for a count of four.

Breathe out for a count of four until your lungs are empty.

Hold your lungs empty for a count of four.

Repeat until you feel your body begin calming down. (For me, it takes about three rounds.)

Studies have shown that "intentional deep breathing can actually calm and regulate the autonomic nervous system . . . reduce stress and improve your mood."[1]

Sometimes calming our anxiety can begin with something as simple as breathing.

God, you formed every part of me, including my fight-or-flight response and nervous system. Help me not to feel shame or guilt over my anxiety but instead to bring everything I feel and all I experience to you. Show me how to deal with my struggles in a way that encompasses every part of me—spiritual, emotional, mental, and physical. Amen.

God Is Bigger Than Your Worry

"Don't worry about this Philistine," David told Saul. "I'll go fight him!"

1 Samuel 17:32

David says to King Saul, "Don't worry." He doesn't say, "There's nothing to worry about." He doesn't dismiss or minimize what's happening. But he also doesn't get stuck in "standstill worry" like the other soldiers.

When fear taunts us, it can seem the most important question is, "How do I stop worrying?" But a more effective one is, "How can I start winning?" After David talks to Saul, he comes up with a plan and then acts. He defeats Goliath with God's help. Instead of being paralyzed by fear, he steps forward in faith.

The story of David and Goliath reminds us giants and worry still can't stand in the face of obedient action and an unstoppable God.

God, thank you that I never have to let worry keep me from victory. When I feel stuck in fear, give me wisdom to evaluate the situation, create a plan, and take the next step of obedience. You are the one writing all of my story. Amen.

God Will Work in You

I am certain that God, who began the good work within you, will continue his work until it is finally finished on the day when Christ Jesus returns.

Philippians 1:6

Our culture tells us we have to constantly improve our lives. But doing so can, ironically, sometimes make them worse. Author Emily Lehman says, "We get into a cycle of constantly 'fixing'—from our mental health to our cleaning supplies, there's always something to fix, with the ideal horizon constantly receding."[1]

Yes, we can make progress, learn, and grow. But if what we thought would improve our lives has become an obstacle to our peace and joy, then it's time to let it go. True transformation comes not from working *on* ourselves but from giving ourselves fully to the God working *in* us.

God, you have freed me from shoulds and invited me into a life of joy. When I'm tempted to place myself under pressure, bring me back to the covering of your grace. I entrust myself to the work you are doing in and through me. Amen.

God Has Promised Victory

So let's not get tired of doing what is good. At just the right time we will reap a harvest of blessing if we don't give up.

Galatians 6:9

When we have a day where we don't make as much progress as we'd hoped, when we feel inadequate for what we're trying to do, when we can't quite seem to understand—let's see it as a sign not of failure but of moving forward. In those moments, it's tempting to criticize ourselves or give up. Instead, we can recognize that we are doing hard work.

We are living with courage.

We are choosing to grow.

We are doing so much better than we know.

God, in the moments when I feel like giving up, help me choose perseverance. In the times when I want to criticize myself, bring me back to grace and your extravagant love. On the days when it seems like I'm failing, remind me that I'm fighting and you have promised victory in the end. I want to learn, grow, and move forward with you for a lifetime. Amen.

God Helps You Run Your Race

Let us run with perseverance the race
marked out for us, fixing our eyes on
Jesus, the pioneer and perfecter of faith.

Hebrews 12:1–2 NIV

We can so quickly shift from focusing on
"the race marked out *for us*" to comparing ourselves with someone else. God invites
us to fix our eyes on the Savior who has gone
before us. If we're focusing on a path besides
our own, let's make sure it's the one that led to
the cross. Because that changes everything.

The path to the cross enables us to "not grow
weary and lose heart" (Heb. 12:3 NIV). It helps us
keep pursuing God's best for us and protects
us from distraction. It also reminds us that the
journey we're on is not about competition but
completion.

These days when I try to be like someone else, I go back to a phrase someone shared with me long ago: "Not my race, not my pace."

God, thank you for the path you have prepared for me and the Savior who has gone before me. I choose not to compare and instead to focus on pursuing you. I will keep my peace. I will honor my pace. I will trust that what you have ahead for me is best. Amen.

God Will Come for You

Come, Lord! The grace of the Lord Jesus
be with you.

1 Corinthians 16:22–23 NIV

Early Christians greeted each other by saying "Maranatha." It's a one-word prayer that means "Come, Lord." And, yes, the ultimate desire behind it is for Jesus to come back and take us Home. But it means much more than that too.

Come, Lord, into the middle of these hard circumstances.

Come, Lord, with your power and peace.

Come, Lord, with your comfort and strength.

God has not left us. He's a God not of distance but devotion, not of neglect but infinite nearness.

God is present in the hardest moments of our lives. He's there in the dark when we whisper prayers. He will never leave or forsake us.

God, sometimes life doesn't turn out the way I'd hoped or planned. Thank you that I can trust you are with me and for me even in those moments. You will never leave me or forsake me. I will never face anything alone. I trust you now. I trust you always. Maranatha. Amen.

God Loves You,
Not Your Productivity

The righteous will flourish like the date
  palm [long-lived, upright and useful];
They will grow like a cedar in Lebanon
  [majestic and stable].
Planted in the house of the LORD,
They will flourish in the courts of our God.

Psalm 92:12–13 AMP

When a tree goes dormant, it releases its leaves, slows its growth, and produces no visible fruit for a time.

We *all* need seasons of dormancy. Maybe we've gone through a time of great growth. Perhaps we're preparing for challenging circumstances. Or we might need to release what's no longer serving God's purposes for our lives.

Whatever the reason, dormancy can feel like a failure rather than a necessity. Shouldn't we produce more, try harder? It's possible to evade dormancy, but it's hard on our souls.

We, like the trees, have our seasons. If God is inviting us into dormancy, we can trust it will not last forever. There will be growth again.

God, you are the Creator of the trees and of my heart. You know the needs of both. Give me the wisdom to embrace all you have for me—times of growth, times of rest. Thank you that my value to you isn't determined by what I produce. Seasons change, but I am always loved the same. Amen.

God Is Your Hope

Why, my soul, are you downcast?
Why so disturbed within me?
Put your hope in God,
for I will yet praise him,
my Savior and my God.

Psalm 42:5 NIV

This morning I became curious about how Psalm 42 ends. I felt surprised to find it closes by repeating *exactly* the same words as the verse above. The psalmist still has the same questions, stresses, and struggles.

This is comforting to me because it reminds me all over again that God isn't expecting us to get over anything. He isn't requiring us to find the perfect cliché that will make our hurt go away. He isn't uncomfortable with the in-between, the places where we are not yet healed.

When we are downcast, we don't have to lift ourselves up; *God will do it*. He is so much more tender with us than we are with ourselves. He lifts up our head like a father does a child with tears streaming down her cheeks. That is why we can say with the psalmist, "I will put my hope in God," even in our worst moments, our hardest times.

God, thank you that you don't expect me to just "cheer up" or force myself to get over anything. Instead, you enter the hard places with me. You are so patient with me. You lift my head not by force but with great gentleness and care. Help me extend the grace you've so freely given me to others. Amen.

God Sees You and Knows You

You are the God who sees me.

Genesis 16:13

Struggles, stresses, ugly attitudes, worries, imperfections. We don't want anyone to see—what would they think of us? We don't want God to see either. We suppose we'd better clean ourselves up and be presentable or risk losing his favor.

We so easily forget that God wants to bring everything into the light. And when he does, it's somehow transformed. The anxiety turns into faith. The fear becomes courage. The worry becomes trust.

We don't ever need to be concerned about what he might find. First, because he already knows it's there. And also because there's nothing his love can't redeem.

God, it's so easy to hide parts of who I am that I'm afraid for you to see. But you already know all of me. Take whatever you find and transform it as only you can. I place all of who I am in your hands. Amen.

God's Love Is Steadfast

Let your steadfast love, O LORD, be upon us,
even as we hope in you.

Psalm 33:22 ESV

The Hebrew word translated here as "stead-fast" means to be "firmly fixed."

When everything in our lives is changing, we can trust in the steadfast love of God. And when we choose to be steady even when it seems there is chaos all around us, we align with that love.

Choosing to be steady requires grit and perseverance, bravery and great strength. It's far easier to just react and do something, anything, because at least then we feel as if we have some control. But realizing all we can really control is our own actions and choices can be a step toward freedom.

And, thankfully, we don't have to be steady by ourselves. We're called to steadfastness because it reflects the heart and character of God.

God, I ask for the courage to be steady even in challenging circumstances. Give me the strength, peace, and resilience I need. I will not let chaos pull me away from your plans for me. Thank you for your steadfast love that I can count on no matter what. Amen.

God Will Never Leave You

God has said, "Never will I leave you; never will I forsake you."

Hebrews 13:5 NIV

We all know the stress of being hurt by another human. These experiences can make us afraid when it seems as if the pain may happen all over again.

Jesus understands because of what he went through on this earth. A dear friend betrayed him to be crucified. Another denied him multiple times. He knew what it felt like to be abandoned, forsaken, and disappointed by those closest to him. Even the best of us are capable of letting down those we love. But we can know, trust, believe, and fully rest our entire selves on the unconditional, unchanging love of God.

Our God is a mender, ever present to make us whole again. He will never leave or forsake us. This is what we can rely on, what we can forever trust.

God, you know what it's like to live in this world and be let down by those you love. When the same happens to me, please draw me close to you and remind me that I am never, ever alone. You are with me and for me in every moment. Give me the courage to keep loving despite the risks. Amen.

God Empowers You to Be a Peacemaker

> Blessed are the peacemakers, for they will be called children of God.
>
> Matthew 5:9 NIV

We can hear "blessed are the peacemakers" and think it's the same as "blessed are the peace*keepers*." But the two are very different.

Making peace means honest communication, grace, compassion, openness about our wants and needs, empathy for the wants and needs of others, a willingness to be vulnerable, patience, and lots of respect. Peacekeeping often means stuffing our feelings, letting ourselves be taken advantage of, allowing harmful behavior to continue, and building up resentment—all of which leads to anxiety.

Sometimes the most valuable, beautiful peace is the kind that comes after a worthwhile battle fought for the sake of love.

God, give me the courage I need to do more than just keep the peace. Instead show me how to be a peacemaker with you. Amen.

God Is with You in Little Moments

Can all your worries add a single moment to your life?

Matthew 6:27

The pie crust I'm rolling out has irregular borders and lumps in various places like tiny mountains. As I work, I remember what the instructor kept saying to us in the pie-making class I attended: "It's only pie."

Fretting over pie crust is just one example of how I sometimes take life far too seriously. I can let myself get worked up over traffic, imagined mistakes, or a conversation that happened months ago. Jesus said, "I tell you not to worry about everyday life—whether you have enough food and drink, or enough clothes to wear. Isn't life more than food, and your body more than clothing?" (Matt. 6:25). In other words, *it's only pie.*

I'm still learning to make peace with the little complications and annoyances of everyday life. But I will practice. I will be patient with myself. I will enjoy the good things that eventually come from the process.

God, you are the one who takes care of every detail of my life. Thank you that I don't have to worry about the little things because you are a big God who loves me. I release all that concerns me to you. Amen.

God's Truth Is Stronger

Overwhelming victory is ours through Christ, who loved us.

Romans 8:37

When we're very tired or stressed out, our inner critic can use words like *disappointment*, *failure*, *bad*. We need to be ready to fight back. So when we hear these words, let's throw back truth in return.

Disappointment.

Daughter of the King.

Failure.

Favored by God.

Bad.

Beloved.

Shame and guilt always try to hold us back from engaging in the battle. But we are promised that when we do fight back, we will win. Because the enemy knows there is nothing stronger than the God who lives within us and the truth he gives us.

God, you are the one who gives me strength, power, and all I need for victory. When the enemy of my heart comes at me with lies, equip me with truth through your Spirit. Give me the courage to fight back, to stand my ground, to never give up or give in. With you, I will always win in the end. Amen.

God's Ways Lead to Joy

As pressure and stress bear down on me,
I find joy in your commands.

Psalm 119:143

This verse sometimes felt like a mystery to me until I realized God's commands come from his heart of love. They are not legalistic human-made standards. The psalmist isn't saying, "As pressure and stress bear down on me, I find joy in your rules." No, instead the meaning is more like, "As pressure and stress bear down on me, I find joy in your ways of love."

When we find joy in God's commands, we live in alignment with his heart and character. We choose to remember we are loved by him no matter our current circumstances or struggles. And we then choose to extend that love to those around us regardless of their imperfections and challenges. We even choose to love our messy, complicated selves in the middle of it all.

It's easy to believe the goal of a command is correction. But, instead, it's connection, which is what we need most during life's hard times.

God, when I think of your commands only in terms of laws, remind me that they are, most of all, about love. In the middle of whatever I'm facing, your ways remain the same. Your character and heart bring me joy and security. I will build my life on who you are and how you care for me. Amen.

God Delights in You

> The very hairs on your head are all numbered. So don't be afraid; you are more valuable to God than a whole flock of sparrows.

> Luke 12:7

Yesterday I refilled the bird feeder, and now it's surrounded by a flock of sparrows. A few finches join in, their wings adding flashes of yellow or red among their plainer cousins. I feed these birds simply because they bring me delight. And according to the psalmist, God feels the same way about us: "For the LORD delights in his people" (Ps. 149:4).

The birds aren't doing anything for me. My delight comes in watching them *be*. This reminds me of how Jesus encouraged his followers to have faith like a child. A child has not yet learned to craft an image or hustle for recognition. For a brief number of years, a child simply *is*. He or she is like the sparrows, who know nothing other than to be true to who they are.

God, give me the courage of the sparrows
and the children. Remind me that I
am loved not because I'm good but
because you are. Help me simply be who
you've created me to be and believe
doing so brings delight to you. Amen.

God Transforms
Your Work

It is useless for you to work so hard
   from early morning until late at night,
anxiously working for food to eat;
   for God gives rest to his loved ones.

Psalm 127:2

The original meaning of the phrase *anxiously working* is "work that hurts." When God spoke the world into being, sculpted a man from clay and a woman from a rib, he made work holy and good. There is work that's sacred and life-giving. But there is another kind of work too—the kind that stresses us out.

The difference between the two is that one comes from a place of fear and the other from a place of love. Our best efforts happen when we believe we're already enough and remember success is about obedience, not outcomes. When we listen to the God who invites us not to labor but to let ourselves be loved.

God, thank you for inviting me not to hustle but to hear your voice. You tell me who I really am and that my worth isn't based on anything I do. Thank you for the gift of work. When I stray from your design for it and let fear take over, calm my anxiety and give me the courage to return to love. Amen.

God Protects
Your Thoughts

The thief's purpose is to steal and kill
and destroy. My purpose is to give them
a rich and satisfying life.

John 10:10

Why do we often remember negative moments more easily than positive ones? Because of the negativity bias we all have. Our brains are wired to give more weight to negative experiences than positive ones and to hold on to them longer. This enables us to learn from mistakes and failures and helps us survive. But left unchecked, our negativity bias can increase our stress and anxiety.

A number of studies have found we need to have five positive thoughts or experiences for every one negative.[1] One way to practice this is to write a prayer each morning listing at least five things you're thankful for from the *previous* day. With a bit of distance and the perspective of a new day, we can often see the treasures our negativity bias might have missed.

God, thank you for how my negativity bias protects me and helps me learn. You gave it to me intentionally for my benefit. When it gets out of balance, help me refocus on what's true, honorable, right, pure, lovely, admirable, excellent, and worthy of praise. Your goodness is present in all of my days. Amen.

God's Peace Guards Your Heart

His peace will guard your hearts and minds as you live in Christ Jesus.

Philippians 4:7

In Philippians 4:6–7, the apostle Paul says when we bring our needs and concerns to God, we'll experience "God's peace, which exceeds anything we can understand."

This kind of peace doesn't cancel out the blood, sweat, and tears of hardships. It doesn't mean we don't feel anger and sadness. It's not a peace where we pretend everything is fine. No, this peace gives us permission to feel all the feelings, to have all the doubts, to experience vulnerability and uncertainty, knowing God will guard our hearts and minds through it all. It's his presence that makes the difference in our lives. It's his love that will get us through whatever we may face.

God, thank you that your peace guards my heart and mind in ways beyond what I can even understand. You are my protector, provider, and the one who gives me true security. Amen.

God Is Your Defender

Guard your heart above all else.

Proverbs 4:23

In Philippians 4:7, the apostle Paul says that God's peace "will guard your hearts and minds as you live in Christ Jesus." God is the one in charge of protecting our hearts. Our role is to stay in an intimate relationship with God and trust him with everything we face. We don't have to live reactively, simply trying to defend our territory. We don't have to hide behind fences of our own making, pretending to be strong.

Instead, we can live in freedom and grace. We can take risks. We can reach out. We can dare to follow our dreams. God's peace will guard our hearts in the process. Each day we can wake up and say, "God, I trust you to take care of me."

Even when life is hard, when the unexpected happens, when we feel vulnerable, we can know that we have a defender.

God, thank you for telling me to guard my heart. Thank you also that I don't have to do it on my own. I can bring everything that concerns me to you, and your peace will be my protection. I trust you with the most tender parts of who I am. Amen.

God Lifts You Up

When anxiety was great within me,
your consolation brought me joy.

Psalm 94:19 NIV

The word *consolation* means "comfort received by a person after a loss or disappointment."[1] God is a friend who consoles us, who wants to hear about our week and our worries, our doubts and discouragement, who will bring us from aching to joy.

There is a kind of comfort that sits with us in the pit. This is good and necessary. But there is another kind that pulls us up out of the pit, that mysteriously takes us from tears to laughing so hard we cry. What if God wants to offer us both? Yes, he is compassionate and gracious, tender with our hearts, and gives us all the time we need to grieve. But he also brings us gifts that delight and inspire us, that remind us life is still beautiful, that surprise us with wonder.

Yes, God is grand and beyond our understanding. But in the darkest moments of life, he is also our friend, the one who knows exactly what will encourage our hearts.

God, thank you that you are with me through it all. When I am anxious, you are a friend who wants to bring me comfort and joy. Help me recognize when you are doing something to support or delight me in the middle of my everyday life. Amen.

God, you are big enough to hold the world in your hands and *loving* enough to care about the smallest details in my life. When I'm anxious, you bring *peace.* When I'm afraid, you give courage. When I'm unsure, you provide confidence. I release my concerns to you now and *entrust* myself to your love. Amen.

God Invites You to a Quiet Life

Make it your goal to live a quiet life, minding your own business and working with your hands, just as we instructed you before.

1 Thessalonians 4:11

Our world today would probably say something like "Make it your goal to live a loud life" or "Make it your goal to live a big life." But all the way back in the early church, Paul had to address the need for a quiet life. He wasn't saying it's bad to be busy. A quiet life is more about the state of our hearts than our schedules.

When my life gets loud, it's usually because I've started comparing. I've gotten away from who God has created me to be and what he has invited me to do. I've stopped listening to the voice of love.

Quiet allows space for my soul to realign with God's heart, even if it's just pausing for a moment to pray when anxiety gets loud.

God, you invite me to lead a quiet life, which is so different from what the world around me says I must do. Give me the courage to choose quiet, and show me what that means for me in this season of my life. I want to listen to your love. Amen.

God's Boundaries Are Wise

May there be peace within your walls
   and prosperity in your palaces.
For the sake of my family and friends, I will say,
   "May you have peace."
For the sake of the house of the LORD our God,
   I will seek what is best for you, O
      Jerusalem.

Psalm 122:7–9

When the psalmist uses the phrase "May there be peace within your walls" (Ps. 122:7), he is talking about the city of Jerusalem, the heart of Israel. But I think these words apply to our hearts too. Like walls, healthy boundaries can protect us and help us have more peace.

In their classic book *Boundaries*, psychologists Henry Cloud and John Townsend write, "Boundaries define us. They define *what is me* and *what is not me*. A boundary shows me where I end and someone else begins, leading me to a sense of ownership. Knowing what I am to own and take responsibility for gives me freedom."[1] We're to accept responsibility for what God has entrusted to us. This includes our feelings, attitudes, beliefs, behaviors, choices, values, limits, talents, thoughts, and desires, as well as our ability to give and receive love.

May there be peace within your walls and within your heart.

God, give me peace within my walls and within my heart. When I need to set a boundary, show me how to do so in ways that are wise, loving, and protective. In Jesus's name, amen.

God Is Always for You

> Such love has no fear, because perfect love expels all fear. If we are afraid, it is for fear of punishment, and this shows that we have not fully experienced his perfect love.
>
> 1 John 4:18

The enemy of our hearts would love for us to believe that when "bad" things happen, we're being punished. But part of the miracle of the gospel is that Jesus took our punishment for us (see Isa. 53:5). Knowing this matters, because otherwise we're tempted to see God as a slightly menacing figure with a lightning bolt in his hand, ready to throw it our way as soon as we do something wrong. But Paul declares, "How much more shall we be saved from God's wrath through him!" (Rom. 5:9 NIV).

God is in our hard times *with* us. He is forever *for* us. We serve a God of love, not lightning bolts. Of mercy, not meanness. Of peace, not punishment.

God, thank you that because of what Jesus did on the cross I don't have to fear punishment. When hard things happen in my life, help me not to ask, "What am I doing wrong?" but instead to remember what Jesus has done for me. You love me, you're for me, and you will make all things right in the end. Amen.

God Offers
You Grace Today

God, have mercy on me, a sinner.

Luke 18:13 NIV

There are two simple prayers we can pray to deter shame. The first is "God, have mercy on me, a sinner." The second is to simply declare, "Jesus is Lord, I am loved, that is all."

There's no case the enemy of your heart can make against those truths. Yes, we *do* sin. But we are also fully forgiven and deeply loved. Your true identity is in what God speaks over you. What Jesus has done on your behalf is irrefutable. His love for you is unchangeable.

We don't have to live in condemnation. We don't have to defend ourselves. We're saints who are new creations, beloved beyond all we can imagine.

God, thank you for your grace that is stronger than any accusation the enemy of my heart may try to bring against me. I don't have to defend myself, because you defend me. Have mercy on me, a sinner. You are Lord, I am loved, that is all. Amen.

God's Peace Can Be Your Peace

I know the LORD is always with me.
I will not be shaken, for he is right
beside me.

Psalm 16:8

Sometimes fear and discomfort can be more of an indicator that we are to do something than a reason to walk away from it. If the human part of me is asking, "Are you out of your mind?" but the Spirit inside is saying, "Trust me anyway," then it's likely a holy prompting.

Instead of saying, "I have peace *about* it," perhaps we can say, "I have peace *within* me." We can have this wild, inexplicable eternal peace even when the future is unsure, our knees are knocking, and our hearts are pounding. It is peace that is beyond our humanity. It is peace only the God of eternity can give.

God, give me wisdom to know your will, courage to take the next step, and discernment to know when peace is external and when it is eternal. I look to you for all I need to get me through whatever I face. Amen.

God Brings You Selah

Meditate within your heart on your bed,
and be still. Selah

Psalm 4:4 NKJV

The word *Selah* appears over seventy times in the book of Psalms, and yet in many ways it remains a mystery. Author and worship pastor Jason Soroski says, "Many commentators think that Selah meant 'to pause' or 'to reflect.' . . . We don't really know for certain."[1]

Selah is placed with intention throughout the Psalms. We can also place it intentionally throughout our days. Selah goes well with morning coffee, prayer closets, and carpool lines. Anywhere we can find a sliver of time. Selah asks only for a deep breath, a few moments, a pause in the middle of the rush. Those little bits of time can make a big difference in our lives much like the meaning of Selah itself—a mystery but deeply true just the same.

God, you invite me not to exhaustion but to intimacy. When I'm tempted to hurry through my days, draw me back to your heart. Show me how to choose peace in not only big ways but also small, everyday ones. Amen.

God Dwells with You

> The Son is the radiance of God's glory and the exact representation of his being.
>
> Hebrews 1:3 NIV

When God sent his Son to earth, the author of Hebrews says he sent his "exact representation," a phrase that means "replica." Every brushstroke, every line and curve the same. Paul tells us that "in Christ all the fullness of the Deity lives in bodily form" (Col. 2:9). God took all of his grandness and mystery, wrapped it in skin, laid it in a manger, walked it through the dusty streets of Jerusalem, hung it from a cross, and raised it from a tomb. He took the eternal and invisible and made it earthly and tangible.

This is the miracle, the truth that's beyond forgery: All of who God is dwelled in Jesus, who dwelled with us, who now dwells in us.

God, you have revealed your heart and character to me through your Son. When I wonder who you are or what you're like, help me remember to look to the replica you gave me of yourself. Jesus alone shows me who you are and how much I'm loved. Amen.

God Calls You to Be Faithful

> The master was full of praise. "Well done, my good and faithful servant. You have been faithful in handling this small amount, so now I will give you many more responsibilities. Let's celebrate together!"
>
> Matthew 25:21

If you're putting pressure on yourself today to do more, be more, achieve more, then pause and take a deep breath. *Just be faithful.* You don't need big resolutions. You don't need to check every item off your bucket list. You don't have to prove your worth. Instead, you can simply say, "Jesus, I will do what I can, where I am, in this moment to love you and others today. Then I will do it again tomorrow."

That's faithfulness.

That's powerful.

That's enough for a lifetime.

God, thank you that you invite me into faithfulness. You're a God not of pressure but peace, not of heaviness but hope, not of relentless striving but relationship. I ask for the courage and wisdom to simply do what I can, where I am, with what I have, to love you and others today. Amen.

God Heals You as You Go

As he entered a village there, ten men with leprosy stood at a distance, crying out, "Jesus, Master, have mercy on us!" He looked at them and said, "Go show yourselves to the priests." And as they went, they were cleansed of their leprosy.

Luke 17:12–14

It's tempting to hold back and stay stuck because we think we have to be completely healed before we "go" and "show." But, as we see in this story from Luke's Gospel, the healing often happens along the way.

We don't have to wait for our healing to be complete before we start moving forward. We don't have to be whole before God sends us out. Of course we want healing to be a onetime, instantaneous event. We can even feel guilty if it's not. But healing is more often a process. Sometimes when we ask God to move, he's asking us the same.

Nothing has the power to hold us back.

We are already worthy.

And God is already at work.

God, thank you that I don't have to be perfect to be part of your plan. You aren't asking me to hold back until my healing is complete. Instead, you invite me to obey today. You give me a path to follow. You are transforming my life with every step. Amen.

God Offers
a New Perspective

Humans do not see what the LORD sees,
for humans see what is visible, but the
LORD sees the heart.

1 Samuel 16:7 CSB

As believers, we can choose to see ourselves and our circumstances from God's perspective. When we find ourselves struggling with our thoughts, we can pause and ask, "God, how do you see me right now? How do you see my circumstances?"

We may worry that God's view of us is judgmental, but "there is no condemnation for those who belong to Christ Jesus" (Rom. 8:1). Because of what Jesus did for us, God looks at us with love and grace. He is relentlessly *for* us. He is looking for our best features—the ones he created, the ones he wants to use for a purpose. He's also looking at our best future, the one beyond our current situation and concerns that he's working out even now.

God, you are the only one who can see it all—past, present, and future. You also see so much deeper than the surface. You see what's eternally true. I want to see myself and my circumstances through your eyes today. Realign my view with yours. Bring me peace through a new perspective. Amen.

God Sees Our Suffering

Now if we are children, then we are heirs—heirs of God and co-heirs with Christ, if indeed we share in his sufferings in order that we may also share in his glory.

Romans 8:17 NIV

Scripture shows us again and again that suffering is part of living in a fallen, broken world. That means when life gets hard, we don't have to say, "I must be doing something wrong." Instead, we can find comfort in knowing that Christ himself faced suffering as he fulfilled his mission.

So we are not to be surprised by suffering; yet we're also not to simply accept it as the way things must be forever. We can ask God, "How are you working even in the midst of this heartache?"

We will have hard days. We will face disappointments. We will experience setbacks. Yet, in the middle of this, we can trust that God's purposes will prevail and we are truly, deeply loved.

God, thank you that I can trust you even in the middle of suffering. Jesus knows what it's like to experience pain, and that's comforting to me. I ask that you give me the strength, courage, and hope I need to move forward no matter what happens in my life. Amen.

God Will Bring Peace on Earth

Glory to God in the highest,
And on earth peace, goodwill toward men!

Luke 2:14 NKJV

Sometimes we forget that Someone already came to save the world. That job has been taken. That task marked complete. It is not on our shoulders. And this is what Jesus told us will continue that mission: "A new command I give you: Love one another" (John 13:34 NIV).

The love of Jesus is how peace on earth, good-will toward men happens.

It's the good news of the gospel.

So let's make this day all about love. All about peace, goodwill toward men. Which is really just another way of saying let's make it all about Jesus.

God, give me the courage to choose grace today. Make me a messenger of peace. A bringer of hope. A reminder that the gospel hasn't changed even if so much in our world is different. You are still speaking, I am still listening. Amen.

God Leads You to Less Worry, More Worship

For the Lord GOD, the Holy One of Israel,
   has said:
"You will be delivered by returning and
   resting;
your strength will lie in quiet
   confidence."

                          Isaiah 30:15 CSB

We serve a God of grace. A God who chases us down right in the middle of all our wild and weary-making running. A God who speaks life and peace and rest into us.

God generously offers us what all tired people need—*rest*. Even if the world around us keeps unavoidably spinning, we can wrap our fingers around peace in a way that truly does pass understanding. And we can let go of all we've grasped that was never meant for us. We can reach out and take hold of the peace that has been promised us today. We can release our striving so we can receive what's infinitely better: God's unconditional love and grace.

God, thank you that you are inviting me today to be not a worker but a worshiper. Thank you that I don't have to hustle, strive, or earn your love. I open my hands and heart to receive the peace and rest you so freely offer me. Amen.

God Is Different and the Same

Jesus Christ is the same yesterday, today, and forever.

Hebrews 13:8

We, as humans, crave both the familiar and the new. Too much of the former and we become bored and restless. Too much of the latter and we're anxious and uncertain.

Thankfully, we serve a God who says, "Behold, I am doing a new thing!" (Isa. 43:19 ESV) and yet "is the same yesterday, today, and forever" (Heb. 13:8). God's heart, character, and ways do not vary. We can count on them not just by the hour but by the minute. But how he shows up, what he brings to us, his mercies and miracles are always brand-new, never repeated.

He is the security we seek. He is the newness we need. He is everything our hearts long for most.

God, you are forever the same and yet always doing something new in my life. In the moments when worry tries to tell me that isn't true, remind me of your character and all the ways you have worked in my life. I believe you are good and mighty, loving and powerful. I trust you with all that concerns me today. Amen.

God Wants You to Take Heart

I have told you these things, so that in me you may have peace. In this world you will have trouble. But take heart! I have overcome the world.

John 16:33 NIV

Here Jesus uses the phrase "take heart" to encourage his followers. This is different from the phrase we use today when we say a person "takes everything to heart."

I've learned that when I take heart in Jesus instead of taking everything to heart, it helps free me from anxiety.

When I take something to heart, I believe it's all on me.

When I take heart in Jesus, I remember he's in control.

When I take something to heart, I feel like I'm alone.

When I take heart in Jesus, I know he will never let me go.

When I take something to heart, I lose my hope.

When I take heart in Jesus, I find him at work even in the hardest circumstances.

Taking heart simply means taking whatever concerns me to Jesus.

Whatever this day brings, I don't have to carry it on my own. I can give it to the only one strong enough to take it. You can too.

God, thank you for giving me a heart that feels deeply. That's your design, and it is good. In the moments when I'm tempted to take everything to heart, help me remember that I can take everything to you instead. You are still in control. You are still taking care of me. You will take care of everyone else too. Amen.

God Knows
Your Emotions

Be angry, and do not sin.

Ephesians 4:26 NKJV

Many of us have learned to stuff anger down as far as it will go. But if we always "keep the peace," then we will never keep our own peace. For others, anger has been a destructive volcano in their life. Either way, say authors Gary Oliver and H. Norman Wright, "You are going to experience anger in your life for many reasons. And when you do, it's important that you face your anger, accept it, hear the message that it is conveying to you, and learn to express your anger in a healthy way. Your anger needs your respect and attention."[1]

When God created our human minds and hearts, he gave us anger along with all the emotions we need to process life. And when we give our anger back to him, he can use it in powerful, healing ways.

God, thank you for my emotions and how each one has a purpose. I ask that you help me understand my anger and use it in the ways you intended. When I'm afraid of anger, give me the courage not to ignore it. When anger tries to control me, give me the strength to yield only to you. Amen.

God's Power Makes You Stronger Every Day

We know that suffering produces perseverance; perseverance, character;
and character, hope.

Romans 5:3–4 NIV

We all have that voice in our lives that tells us the way to handle stress is by having another drink, buying one more thing we don't need, or burying our feelings at the bottom of a gallon of ice cream. "You should never feel bad," it tells us. "You can make all the hurt go away right now."

Each time we choose not to listen to that voice, it's hard and it hurts. But next time we can per-severe longer. Over time, this actually changes who we are, our character. We get stronger and know we can handle more, which brings hope.

You've done more than you thought you could. You didn't give up. You showed up and gave it your best today. And that's enough to make you stronger for tomorrow.

God, when I'm tempted to choose what weakens me, fill me with the power I need to persevere. I will not give up. I am getting stronger every day. Amen.

God's Courage Can Be Yours

Peter went over the side of the boat and walked on the water toward Jesus. But when he saw the strong wind and the waves, he was terrified and began to sink. "Save me, Lord!" he shouted.

Jesus immediately reached out and grabbed him. "You have so little faith," Jesus said. "Why did you doubt me?"

When they climbed back into the boat, the wind stopped.

Matthew 14:29–32

In this biblical story, Peter decides to take a risk. We often stop the story when Peter begins to sink and Jesus reaches out his hand to save him. But look at what happens next: "When they climbed back into the boat, the wind stopped."

Peter *did* successfully walk on water. He walked with Jesus all the way back to the boat! And when they made it, the storm subsided.

When you dare to take that step of faith despite your fear, it may be the very thing that brings you closer to Jesus, lets you experience more than you ever imagined with him, and perhaps even leads you to the moment when the storm finally subsides.

God, I thank you that you have more in store for me than I can even imagine. I sense that you are asking me to take a step of faith by _____. Please give me the courage to step out and come to you. Amen.

God Will Take the Next Step with You

For the joy set before him he endured the cross.

Hebrews 12:2 NIV

Author and researcher Marcus Buckingham did a study with thousands of women to discover what made them thrive. The results were surprising because external factors didn't matter. The women who thrived spent more time each day in moments that made them feel stronger, that led them toward more joy in the long term.[1]

It's okay to pause and look at what's draining or discouraging you. It's necessary to let go of what continually diminishes your soul. You are wise, not weak, to be intentional with your experiences, emotions, and energy. It's responsible to release what God never intended you to carry so you can move forward in love and freedom.

Dare to start asking, "What's the joy set before me?" Then take the next brave step God has for you without guilt, shame, or apology.

God, show me how to look for the joy set before me so that it will help me persevere through what I'm facing now. If what I'm moving toward isn't your will or your way for me, help me know that too and turn in a new direction. Amen.

God Helps You Stand Firm

For shoes, put on the peace that comes
from the Good News so that you will be
fully prepared.

Ephesians 6:15

The peace that comes from God is fierce and mighty, unmovable and unstoppable. It "comes from the Good News." It's the peace that reminds us God is on our side and we will be victorious no matter what. Peace is not simply an emotion. Peace is a position we take of standing on who God is, what he has promised, and who he tells us we are.

How do we put on the shoes of peace? By standing firm on what's true regardless of how we feel or what's happening around us. The enemy of our hearts knows he can't defeat us. His only hope is convincing us to retreat.

Instead, we can dig in and refuse to move. We can stay steady and never give an inch. We can remember, "The LORD will fight for you; you need only to be still" (Exod. 14:14 NIV).

God, you are the one who enables me to stand firm and be brave. It seems like a paradox that peace is what I need for battle, but it's true. No matter what's going on around me, keep me steady and grounded in you. Amen.

God Tells
the Truest Stories

Think sensibly, as God has distributed a
measure of faith to each one.

Romans 12:3 CSB

We all know kids' perceptions don't always reflect reality. But we forget the same is true for us as adults. When we navigate a stressful situation and tell ourselves, "I'm going to fail. Everyone is annoyed with me. I have no idea what I'm doing," that is not reality, just our perception.

We can dwell on all that has gone wrong. We can pretend everything is fine. Or we can pause and ask God to help us find a different version of our story.

Here's the secret: As humans, we naturally create fiction. God is the only one who can help us live in truth. He is still writing history. He is still writing your story too. He alone holds the pen that gets to write "The End."

God, you are the way, the truth, and the life. When my thoughts and emotions don't align with what's true, show me a different version of the story—one that leads to hope and moving forward in faith. I trust your words and your work. Amen.

God Calls You His Child

> We are citizens of heaven, where the Lord Jesus Christ lives. And we are eagerly waiting for him to return as our Savior.
>
> Philippians 3:20

You are a child of God, someone loved beyond all you can imagine. *No matter what.* Life's obstacles are temporary. Who you are is eternal.

Your circumstances may change, but who you truly are remains forever the same.

When we're in the middle of a bad day or a hard season, we can lean into God's heart and ask, "Who am I *in spite of this*? Tell me what's true about me no matter what happens."

Hebrews reassures us that "it is impossible for God to lie" (6:18). Your circumstances will lie to you. Your emotions will lie to you. Even other people will lie to you. But not God.

God, nothing that happens to me in
this life can change who you say I am.
My identity is secure in you forever.
On the days when I'm tempted to
believe where I am is who I am,
remind me of what is true. Amen.

God Created You for a Purpose

We are God's handiwork, created in Christ Jesus to do good works, which God prepared in advance for us to do.

Ephesians 2:10 NIV

Before we ever came into being, God had a purpose in mind for us. As he alone watched our bodies being formed in our mothers' wombs, he already knew what was ahead.

Just because your circumstances are hard doesn't mean God's purpose for you has changed. God's purpose for you *will* prevail. In all of history, no person has ever been able to thwart God's ultimate plan. He can redeem and reroute as much as is needed to get you to the destination he has in mind.

That's the secret: You don't have to carry the load of living with purpose. You can embrace it, celebrate it, cling to it—but you don't have to make it happen. God is going to use you in unexpected, powerful ways.

God, sometimes life is messy and I don't understand what's happening or how it will all work out. But I'm yours. Thank you for creating me with a purpose. Thank you that nothing and no one can destroy that purpose. You will make sure it's fulfilled. Amen.

God Brings Strength in Weakness

If I must boast, I would rather boast about the things that show how weak I am.

2 Corinthians 11:30

You may think you have nothing to offer. But still God asks, "Will you let me use you, right here and right now?"

Your weaknesses and struggles are not reasons for him to give up on you. Instead, they're opportunities for you to show his strength in ways you simply can't on your best days.

The very places and times when you feel God can use you least are when he may actually shine through you most.

God, sometimes I don't feel like I have much to give. But you are in me during those times just as you are in the moments when I feel the strongest and most capable. I want the world to receive what you have designed me to share. I yield myself to you. Use all I have to make much of you. Amen.

God Offers
a Life of Love

So now I am giving you a new commandment: Love each other. Just as I have loved you, you should love each other.

John 13:34

We are made to connect with others. And when we bring joy to others, it comes back to us in both spiritual and physical ways.

Throughout Scripture, God uses messy, broken people right in the middle of their greatest challenges. We don't need to have it all together. Wherever we are today, we can serve in some way. Even if it's just offering a smile to the nurse in our hospital room. Or making our toddler giggle when we're almost at the end of our patience. Or listening to a friend at church on Sunday morning when we'd really like to get home to our house and the couch instead.

Many times we won't know the impact on this side of heaven. But all of the little things add up to a lifetime of resilience and loving well.

God, I'm grateful that I don't have to go through life alone, that you created me to connect with others and share my burdens with them. Show me who I can encourage today, and help me reach out when life is stressful and I need encouragement too. Amen.

God Helps When You're Overwhelmed

> I cry to you for help
> when my heart is overwhelmed.
>
> Psalm 61:2

What helps when you're overwhelmed? First, you can cry out to God as the psalmist says. Then you can assist your nervous system in calming down. One way to do that is to focus on the present moment. Try the following technique recommended by many mental health experts.

Pause and notice . . .

- 5 things you see (example: sky)
- 4 things you feel (example: mug)
- 3 things you hear (example: music)
- 2 things you smell (example: lotion)
- 1 thing you taste (example: coffee)

Having times when you become overwhelmed is part of being human, but you can learn to manage them. And you don't have to do it alone.

Pause today and recognize that being overwhelmed doesn't mean you're weak. It means you have given absolutely everything you've got. Now it's time to give yourself what you need too.

God, I'm so grateful that I, like the psalmist, can cry out to you when I'm overwhelmed. Give me the discernment to know my limits and the courage to honor them, trusting when I do so, it's not weakness but wisdom. Amen.

God's Grace Changes Your Goals

Do not despise these small beginnings, for the LORD rejoices to see the work begin.

Zechariah 4:10

When we set goals, we often act as if they're going to happen in isolation from the rest of our lives. We think of what we could do if we had no other challenges or responsibilities. But when we set goals, it's important to consider one additional factor—our current level of life stressors. Then *we can match our goal level with our life-stressor level.*

Life requires us to continually adapt, change, grow, slow down, speed up, try again. So if we're going to set goals, we need a perspective that works the same way.

God's goal for our lives isn't perfection; it's growth and connection. Every effort counts. Every step matters. Every little bit of progress can be reason for rejoicing.

God, you have no trouble with your to-do list. There is no goal you can't instantly reach. That means what matters most to you isn't how much I can do but my relationship with you. When I try to push too hard, remind me I have nothing to prove. Help me rejoice in small beginnings with you. Amen.

God Frees You to Let Go of Expectations

Be silent before the LORD and wait
expectantly for him.

Psalm 37:7 CSB

Scripture shows us how we can live *expectantly* instead of wearing ourselves out with *expectations*. What's the difference? Expectations are of our own making; living expectantly means opening ourselves to what God will do.

Isn't faith really the ultimate example of living expectantly? The Jewish people expectantly watched for a Messiah. Mary and Joseph expectantly waited for Jesus to be born. The wise men expectantly followed the star.

This is my simple prayer for whatever season I'm in: *God, give me the courage to let go of expectations and live expectantly.* Will you pray this with me?

God, I will say it again—give me the courage to let go of expectations and live expectantly. You alone know the future. You hold the whole world, and my little life, in your hands. When I'm tempted to give in to demands you never placed on me, remind me of what is true and set me free. Amen.

God's Love Is New Every Morning

Because of the LORD's great love we are
     not consumed,
   for his compassions never fail.
They are new every morning;
   great is your faithfulness.

                    Lamentations 3:22–23 NIV

Whenever we make it through a stressful moment in life, isn't that a new morning full of God's mercy? Psalm 30:5 says, "Weeping may last through the night, but joy comes with the morning."

We experience mourning, yes, but we are ultimately people of the morning. Even when the story ends in tragedy, it is only for this life. We have a forever morning coming.

No matter how hard this world gets, we keep finding our way through the dark. We keep moving toward the light. We keep believing that what looks like an ending could really be a beginning.

A new morning is always coming. The sun will rise again, and so will we.

God, you have seen everything that has ever happened on this earth. You know how dark the night can get. Yet you bring light again every day to this world, to my life. Thank you for the gift of new starts and unending hope. No matter what comes, the morning will too. Amen.

God Will Make All Things Right in the End

> He will wipe every tear from their eyes, and there will be no more death or sorrow or crying or pain. All these things are gone forever.
>
> Revelation 21:4

This moment when God wipes all the tears from our eyes will also be the end of our anxiety. We will never again experience fear. We'll live with complete peace, joy, and love. We catch glimpses of that in this life, perhaps when we're laughing with friends on a summer evening, holding a baby in our arms, watching a bird soar or a dolphin swim. They're moments when we're caught up in something bigger and wilder than we are, when the critical voice inside us goes silent in awe.

In heaven, we will live like this always. Close your eyes and imagine it for a moment. Between now and then, we're all just on a journey Home. This is only the beginning. God has so much more for you, in this life and in eternity. Until then, remember that you are God's beloved.

God, thank you for the journey I'm on with you. I look forward to the joyful day when I'm forever free of anxiety. Until then, I will keep moving forward one step at a time with you. Amen.

NOTES

God Gives You a New Song

1. Yana Hoffman and Hank Davis, "Sing in the Shower to Make Friends with Your Vagus Nerve," *Psychology Today*, March 17, 2020, https://www.psychologytoday.com/us /blog/try-see-it-my-way/202003/sing-in-the-shower-make -friends-your-vagus-nerve.

God Equips You to Handle Anything

1. *Old and New Testament Greek Lexical Dictionary*, under "Strong's #842," accessed January 4, 2022, https://www .studylight.org/lexicons/eng/greek/842.html.

God Gets You Through Stress to Joy

1. Kelly McGonigal, *The Upside of Stress: Why Stress Is Good for You, and How to Get Good at It* (Penguin, 2016), 64.

God Transforms Being Anxious

1. Olga Khazan, "Can Three Words Turn Anxiety into Suc-cess?," *The Atlantic*, March 23, 2016, https://www.theatlantic .com/health/archive/2016/03/can-three-words-turn-anxi ety-into-success/474909/.

God Brings You True Peace

1. Timothy Keller, "The Meaning of Shalom in the Bible," New International Version (website), accessed December 7, 2020, https://www.thenivbible.com/blog/meaning-shalom-bible/.

God Can Shift Your Perspective

1. Martin E. P. Seligman, Susan Nolen-Hoeksema, and Joan S. Girgus, "Learned Helplessness in Children: A Longitudinal Study of Depression, Achievement, and Explanatory Style," *Journal of Personality and Social Psychology* 51, no. 2 (1986): 435–42.

God Provides Satisfaction for Your Soul

1. Susan Schoenian, "Feeding and Watering Equipment," Sheep 201: A Beginner's Guide to Raising Sheep, accessed December 7, 2020, http://www.sheep101.info/201/feedwaterequip.html.

God Gives You Breath

1. Ana Gotter and Dr. Debra Rose Wilson, "Box Breathing," HealthLine, June 17, 2020, https://www.healthline.com/health/box-breathing#steps.

God Will Work in You

1. Emily Lehman, "Optimize Now: The Never-Ending Pursuit of the Perfect Lifestyle," Verily, January 13, 2020, https://verilymag.com/2020/01/daily-routines-obsession-optimizing-apps-technology-burnout-culture.

God Protects Your Thoughts

1. Hara Estroff Marano, "Our Brain's Negativity Bias," *Psychology Today*, June 9, 2016, https://www.psychologytoday.com/us/articles/200306/our-brains-negative-bias.

God Lifts You Up

1. *Lexico*, under "consolation," accessed February 1, 2021, https://www.lexico.com/definition/consolation.

God's Boundaries Are Wise

1. Henry Cloud and John Townsend, *Boundaries: When to Say Yes, How to Say No to Take Control of Your Life* (Zondervan, 2017), 31.

God Brings You Selah

1. Jason Soroski, "What Does Selah Mean in the Bible and Why Is It Important?," Crosswalk.com, October 10, 2018, https://www.crosswalk.com/faith/bible-study/what-does-selah-mean.html.

God Knows Your Emotions

1. Gary J. Oliver and H. Norman Wright, *Good Women Get Angry: A Woman's Guide to Handling Her Anger, Depression, Anxiety, and Stress* (Servant Publishing, 1996), 13–14.

God Will Take the Next Step with You

1. Marcus Buckingham, *Find Your Strongest Life: What the Happiest and Most Successful Women Do Differently* (Thomas Nelson, 2009), 88.

HOLLEY GERTH loves humans, words, and good coffee. She's a *Wall Street Journal* bestselling author, master life coach, and cohost of the *More than Small Talk* podcast. Her background also includes being a counselor and cofounding one of the  first online communities for Christian women. Holley is passionate about helping people embrace who they are and become all they're created to be. You can connect with her and find more resources at HolleyGerth.com.

CONNECT WITH HOLLEY

HolleyGerth.com

  @HolleyGerth